motivating
reluctant readers

Alfred J. Ciani, Editor
University of Cincinnati

INTERNATIONAL READING ASSOCIATION
800 Barksdale Road   Newark, Delaware 19711

INTERNATIONAL READING ASSOCIATION

Copyright 1981 by the
International Reading Association, Inc.

Library of Congress Cataloging in Publication Data

International Reading Association.
 Motivating reluctant readers.

 Six of the nine articles were presented at a
preconvention institute held at the twenty-third
annual convention of the International Reading
Asociation, Houston, Texas, May 1978.
 1. Reading—Congresses. 2. Motivation in
education—Congresses. 3. Children—Books and
reading. I. Ciani, Alfred J., 1946-
II. Title.
LB1049.95.I57 1981   428.4   80-25199
ISBN 0-87207-530-3
Second Printing, September 1983

Contents

As nourishers of learning, we need to seize upon any vehicle which may enhance this process.—Lori Fisk/Henry Clay Lindgren, *Learning Centers*, 1974

Foreword

Young people who can't read (anything) are far outnumbered by young people who can read (at least some things) but don't. Can we motivate reluctant readers? I believe we can. If reading instruction employed only genuine materials, and recognized only valid purposes, very few young people could resist the pressing need—even the burning desire—to read. In other words, reading programs built on the understanding that genuine materials *will* be read for valid purposes could well make nonreaders an endangered species.

Valid purposes refers to those universal human needs and individual human interests which are best satisfied through the use of language in general, and printed language in particular. Examples of these needs and interests are evident in the language functions enumerated by M.A.K. Halliday. They include:

- the "I want" function of fulfilling needs
- the "Don't do that" function of controlling or regulating
- the "Me and you" function of relating to others
- the "This is me" function of defining self
- the "Tell me why" function of finding out
- the "Let's pretend" function of making believe
- the "I've got something to tell you" function of communicating about content.

Genuine materials, on the other hand, are materials written in order to satisfy one or more valid purposes, such as the language functions listed above. Whether published for the public at large, or scrawled for personal reasons only, they are almost always meant to be read. They include:

- trade books, newspapers, and magazines

- free or inexpensive materials designed to inform, promote, or persuade
- material written, adapted, or constructed by a teacher
- oral and written expressions of young people themselves.

Genuine materials for reading instruction are represented perhaps least of all by texts, basal readers, workbooks, kits, filmstrips, and television programs specially contrived for the express purpose of teaching reading.

This International Reading Association volume, as edited by Alfred J. Ciani, contains articles which were first presented to professionals in reading at IRA's annual convention held in Houston in 1978. Three additional articles were prepared especially for this publication. The edited volume, *Motivating Reluctant Readers*, clearly reflects the viewpoint expressed above. The contributors suggest an additional component, also: that is, the essential role performed by sensitive and knowledgeable adults, those who encourage and participate in reading and writing throughout the school, in the home, and beyond.

I recommend *Motivating Reluctant Readers*.

Richard A. Earle
McGill University

Preface

The majority of articles collected in this monograph were the result of a Preconvention Institute held at the Twenty-third Annual Convention of the International Reading Association, Houston, Texas, May 1978. After initial review, Lloyd Kline, IRA Director of Publications, suggested that I review additional manuscripts to make this monograph more complete. As a result, three additional articles were selected for inclusion. The total work represents views on many facets of why some youngsters refuse to read and what may be done to get them to *want* to read. Thus, *Motivating Reluctant Readers* provides suggestions for working with those students who function at a frustration level and those who have an aversion to reading.

AJC

Introduction

Terry Bullock
University of Oregon

Most students are involved in reading tasks for a major portion of their school day. Outside the school environment many functional tasks require some sort of reading—ranging from learning to toast Pop Tarts, to deciding which bus to take, to selecting from the TV guide a television program to view. Teachers of reading work very hard at their profession. Many parents require their children to do some reading every day. Many even let their children *catch* them enjoying reading at home. Local, state, and federal agencies allocate millions of dollars to their education budgets. Why, then, does there seem to be a problem in teaching students how to read and stimulating them to *want* to read?

In *Developmental Reading: A Psycholinguistic Perspective*, Hittleman suggests that reading is acquired through interaction with the materials, the teacher, and the environment. This can be interpreted as a framework on which classroom and reading teachers may begin to improve reading achievement among their students. These three factors, then, deserve additional scrutiny.

It seems difficult to place blame on the materials as a cause of failure to want to learn to read. Today, the development and production of commercially prepared materials is a multimillion dollar business; the variety of materials is extensive. The difficulty seems to be one of matching appropriate materials to learners.

Persons matching materials to the learners then may be the cause of reading problems. Yet those persons, the teachers,

1

are prepared in preservice programs founded on a theoretical framework which has been supported through years of empirical investigation. In addition, field placements in which preservice persons participate help to make methods courses more meaningful.

Interaction with the environment? It seems that youngsters today have many "irons in the fire." That is, young people are involved in hobbies and recreational activities, many of which didn't even exist twenty years ago.

Another factor which may cause reading problems seems to be the students. Yet, everytime I speak to a group of first graders, they all seem motivated to learn to read. What happens between grades one and six? Is there really an iatrogenic problem as the article by Beverly Farr suggests?

If student motivation is so high and we are preparing teachers based on the best methods, and the materials are better today than they have ever been, what causes reading problems?

There is no simple answer. There are, however, many strategies which could be considered. The following collection of articles provides help to classroom teachers, reading clinicians, and parents. It is a refreshing look at how to turn kids on to reading. Yet, this is only the beginning—the next steps are up to the readers of these pages.

What is important is that language and experience, examined experience, play an enormously important role not only in the way reading develops into critical comprehension but also in the way logical thinking develops.—Russell G. Stauffer, *The Language Experience Approach to the Teaching of Reading*, 1980

Building Language Experiences for Reluctant Readers

Beverly P. Farr
Indiana University

Acquiring language is a very complex task for the young child. The natural process by which one does it can suggest ways to develop language experiences in the classroom which will enable the reluctant reader, as well as other students, to improve both the skill of reading and attitudes toward reading.

Problems of the Reluctant Reader

What makes a reader reluctant? Most educators would agree that a child is reluctant to read for one of two reasons: either the child is unable to read and unwilling to try because of a history of unsuccessful attempts or is able to read but not motivated to do so. This explanation leads to two questions more difficult to answer: Why is a child unable to learn to read? How can a child be motivated to read? The first question, which has no definitive answer, has been a source of controversy over the years. Most educators conclude that a combination of causes contributes to a reading disability. More attention seems to be given, however, to intellectual causes such as low IQ or inadequate reasoning ability, and to physiological causes, grouped for the most part under the general category of learning disability. Less attention is given to emotional problems (since it is difficult to tell when such problems cause reading failure and when they are a result of a failure to learn to read) and educational problems such as the mismatch of instructional approach and learner style.

Several other factors are given little attention, primarily because it is virtually impossible to prove their contribution to the problem. These factors may be most significant, however, in that they are probably most amenable to specific remediation, i.e., it is possible to alter classroom strategies and, thereby, eliminate the negative effect of the factors.

The first factor may be identified as a misconception of the reading process that some children develop as a result of instructional procedures used. The fear that children will not learn all the basic skills prompts teachers to use a variety of materials and activities which endorse the practice of isolated skills and the belief that such practice will lead to better reading. As Maracek (5) states, "When skills take over... and word recognition becomes an end in itself, there is a greater dislike for the whole reading process. Instead of opening up the world of literature as a source of pleasure, reflection, and insight, we close the door to enjoyment and exploration—the primary goals of reading." As a consequence of skill-oriented instruction or an overemphasis on word recognition, some children are lured away from the idea that reading is a meaning-getting process. They see reading as a "subject," one in which they are continually meeting failure. At the same time, teachers who adopt a skill-oriented, word-focused concept (particularly regarding the learning-to-read process) often misevaluate a child's reading and give the impression that the youngster is a poor reader when, in fact, s/he may have developed some profitable strategies (often in spite of instruction).

Another factor which may contribute to a reading problem is the lack of sufficient background information to enable a child to deal with the concepts, situations, or events included in the printed material. Much is taken for granted regarding the knowledge children bring to the printed page.

A third factor involves the presentation in school of material that is often meaningless and uninteresting to a child. It does not command the child's attention because it is not personally important. Lack of interest may be the single greatest cause of failure to learn.

These three factors may be considered *iatrogenic* problems. The term, "iatrogenic," is most commonly used by the medical profession as it means "induced inadvertently by a physician or his treatment." It can be applied to the field of education when children have failed to learn to read as an indirect result of instructional procedures used in the schools, not because of problems inherent in the children. It means that many children have not learned to read as a result of the educational "treatment" they received because the treatment was inadequate, misdirected, or inappropriate.

To summarize, instructional procedures used to teach reading as a subject may be inherently bad for the following reasons:

1. A skill-oriented, word-focused approach leads chilren away from the essential understanding that reading is a meaning-getting process. Furthermore, when evaluation of children's reading is based on a misconception of the process, positive strategies they may have developed go unnoticed.
2. Sufficient background information and the ability to manipulate the concepts from a piece of material often are not adequately developed prior to reading.
3. Materials used may not be interesting or important to individual children. They may see no purpose in performing tasks other than because they are assigned.

Some children do not learn to read and, thus, develop considerable anxiety over a history of failure. At the junior high level, the inability to read carries substantial negative impact. Other students have some ability and are unaware of it. Still others are able to read quite well and do not choose to do so because reading has not been presented as an interesting, exciting, meaningful activity.

Learning Language

Certain aspects of the language-learning process in young children present information applicable to the process of learning to read. This information points to the need for certain revisions in the curriculum, revisions which would enable children to perceive reading and writing to be as meaningful as speaking and listening.

Children develop language only within the context of meaningful usage. Language develops as a result of an increasing awareness of the functions of language. As children's awareness of what can be done with language increases, two things happen. Their language develops, and their views of the world develop. As a result, children have personalized views of the world and a tool (language) that can be used to cope with the world and tell others about it. By learning to use language, children bring to the classroom a basic understanding of language and of the world. Children also have a basic understanding of what language can do (4). As children interact and use language in a wide variety of situations, an awareness of the world and an increasingly greater ability to understand continue to develop.

It has also been substantiated that children who are learning language understand only that for which they have sufficient background information. Furthermore, they cannot repeat what they don't understand, i.e., comprehension precedes production.

It is known that motivation and interest always have substantial impact on the learning of any task; but this is, perhaps, nowhere more evident than in the acquisition of language. Spread before children like an incomparable smorgasbord of new delights, the world begs to be put into words. Children's natural curiosity constantly meets something new—objects, experiences, feelings—and they seek to identify them for themselves and others.

The role adults play in the acquisition of language by young children also has implications for classroom learning. Adults continually point out new things to children and provide linguistic information regarding new experiences. When it is necessary, they supply background information to help children deal with new concepts. Most significantly, they are accepting of children's struggling attempts to use language, reinforcing those attempts and generally supporting the risk-taking behavior necessary for the learning of such a complex task. In essence, adults make it as easy as possible for children. As a result, children are not reluctant to make the effort.

In discussing the acquisition of language and implications for the classroom, Cazden (1) states, "As far as we can tell now, all that the child needs is exposure to well-informed sentences in the context of conversation that is meaningful and sufficiently personally important to command attention. Implications for how to help children continue their learning in school are far less certain [but]... the most obvious implication is that teachers should act the way parents have acted: talk with children about topics of mutual interest in the context of the child's ongoing work and play." Knowing how children learn language should help us to design better classroom situations that permit them to extend this learning.

Experiencing Language in the Classroom

Although children have acquired all of the basic language structures by the time they are five years old, the uses to which they put language continue to be refined and developed throughout their lifetime. An experience centered approach wherein the language arts skills are integrated— reading is seen as a tool, a skill employed for the sake of some larger activity—can prevent the development of the iatrogenic problems discussed earlier. This approach will allow children to identify a purpose for reading and, when carefully planned with substantive input from children, can be highly motivating. The inclusion of a wide variety of types and levels of materials and activities allows students—otherwise reluctant because they are afraid of failure—to experience success, an experience which is mandatory if progress is the goal. The approach also contributes to the development of the conceptual background necessary for comprehension.

The classroom teacher can play a significant role in helping children develop language by structuring the classroom in such a way that what is to be learned is meaningful; activities must allow for the use of language in various contexts. Much of what goes on in the classroom today is meaningless to children. It is artificial and bears little resemblance to real-life activities. The situation must be reversed so the children are able to perceive the usefulness of what they are learning; they need to understand the purpose. Many children learn to say words accurately or to answer "who, what, where," and even "what might have been, what do you think" questions without ever developing a clear notion of the purpose for reading. As a result, they do not participate voluntarily in reading on a routine basis and, therefore, do not use this channel to develop language or to develop their ideas about the world.

A manifest need to read or write for some purpose is not naturally present in the classroom. Many text writers try to assist teachers in the task of bringing about believable situations calling for reading or writing, but the text often lacks relevancy and the immediacy of materials containing information, ideas, or feelings sought by potential readers at any particular time. The *Guinness Book of Records* or the latest issue of *Popular Mechanics* may be of greater potential interest and a greater stimulation to learning at certain moments than any prescribed reading book (2).

Reading must be functional for the reader. People read in order to make their world more understandable, sensible, and ordered. A reading program based on this concept provides opportunities for students to read for purposes which are important to them and to make order and sense of their world (3). If situations are designed in the classroom where the student is intimately involved—situations which are meaningful and concrete, which utilize the student's language and build on the information brought to the printed page—the predictability of the material is increased and the student experiences greater success and greater enjoyment.

Elements of the Plan

The rationale for such a program is important, but more important is to consider what such a classroom would look like and to suggest ways to put such a program into practice. The first step is to conceive of an overall framework into which a wide variety of activities can be integrated. A thematic approach can be used effectively with junior and senior high school students, and especially with those students who are having problems with reading and are "turned off" to typical classroom texts and activities. In a classroom where themes are the focus rather than skills, all skills deemed essential develop within the natural context of meaningful application. The theme is a focal point or an area of interest or study. The factor of interest is a crucial one, and the teacher should determine themes with considerable input from the students. If an interest can be maximized or created, it will serve as an indispensable vehicle for learning. Individuals are more willing to read about or write about experiences that have been stimulating or interesting to them. The list of themes is endless; some will be of greater interest to junior high students. Presented in a creative manner, however, some topics will unexpectedly stimulate interest. The teacher can determine the various situations and classroom groupings that can be used to explore each theme. Situations may range from weather reports to dramatic interpretations to model construction. Work on the theme may be carried out on an independent basis, or as a total group, or may involve interactions among small groups.

Let's say that a teacher and the students in a junior high classroom decide to study television. It's important initially to make something happen. Students then have something about which they can speak, write, listen, and read. In this case, a visit to a television station or a prepared viewing of a television program might serve as the initial experience. The class decides that they want to explore such questions as: How are ratings determined? What are favorite programs among various age groups? How was television developed? How has television programing changed over the years? What evidence is there that television has a negative effect on human behavior? How are commercials written? These questions can be organized into areas of study.

In order to narrow a theme into several topics of interest, the teacher might use a "web of interest" as suggested by Norton (6). As an example, Norton cites a class which had chosen the general theme of "water." A web was drawn on the blackboard to ascertain the various subjects that might be investigated around the central theme. Five broad topics were discussed: the water cycle, experiments, fresh water, water power, and oceans. Each water-based topic was then broken down into more defined subtopics. In the television topic cited, broad topics based on the questions given might include: history, production, programing, viewing habits, and commercials. Students interested in specific subtopics can be identified and assigned to various interest groups.

Together, the teacher and interest groups can then determine the activities that will help them explore the theme. Presenting simulated television programs of various types, writing commercials, researching television programing or its history, conducting surveys or interviews, reading scripts, making television games, reading fiction and nonfiction about television, building a mock television studio, or listening to a guest speaker from the world of television are a few of the numerous activities possible that will call upon the need to listen, speak, read, and write.

One of the significant advantages of such a plan is that student interests within a subject area—rather than reading ability—are the basis for grouping, and it is possible to differentiate instruction through the inclusion of appropriate materials at a number of reading ability levels. Poor readers are able to investigate at their own levels while also receiving information and motivation from interaction with the more accelerated members of an interest group. Through the choice of subtopics that interest them and the opportunity to present their findings to an appreciative audience, readers at all abilities are stimulated. In these groups, students may be encouraged to plan together, discuss together, and present their information to the class. The groups thus furnish a vehicle for the total integration of the language arts (6).

When a theme is expanded into a wide variety of situations and activities, not only do students develop the various uses of language, they also can develop skills in research, discussion, organization, dramatics, graphics, and presentation. Norton's classroom description (6) serves as a good example of how a theme can be explored:

> The groups met together to plan, read about, and discuss their findings. Each group had the responsibility of presenting information to the total class. This requirement provided motivation for research and an excellent vehicle for the application of language arts skills. In addition, the reporting provided all ability levels in the class with valuable information. The class developed and applied reference, writing, discussion, creative, dramatic, organizing and listening skills. The interest group investigating water pollution, for example, wrote a TV script incorporating ecology commercials to present the information. The ocean exploration group developed an interview that could be conducted with a famous scientist, including questions about problems which the group had researched. The group had to investigate many sources in order to formulate answers they felt the scientist would utilize in question responses.

The water experimentation group made graphs and drawings to illustrate the results of their experiments. They maintained a diary to show experimental progress and finally presented an experiment as part of their oral report.

The group investigating the production of electricity prepared a "movie" showing how electricity is obtained from water. The water cycle group made transparencies and used an overhead projector to present their information. Pictures of cloud formations were included as well as pictures that showed the influences of the water cycle on geography.

Using a thematic approach as the framework, a teacher can easily develop a variety of language experiences which will integrate the language arts and present them as purposeful activities, stimulate the interest of the reluctant reader, supply necessary background information, and provided opportunities for success. Of course, not all classroom time can be spent in a plan that includes various activities related to a theme. It should be emphasized, however, that other classroom activities should be based on the natural and meaningful use of language as much as possible. If materials and activities make sense, are of interest, and permit success, they will attract all students, including those who are reluctant to read. All so-called language arts skills are better taught in situations where skills are applied in a purposeful way. Writing for a class newspaper, leading a discussion on a topic of interest, developing an easy-to-read automobile manual, publishing class books, designing greeting cards, listing questions for a guest speaker, participating in an interview or panel discussion, or keeping a journal are all activities that allow for the use of language in meaningful ways. Such activities will make the classroom a place where students are interested in what they are doing, are learning by being involved in concrete experiences, are using language in meaningful ways, and are discovering the world through reading.

References

1. CAZDEN, COURTNEY B. "Suggestions from Studies of Early Language Acquisition," *Childhood Education*, 45 (December 1969), 127-131.
2. EVANS, PETER O. "Reading As an Integrated Learning Activity," *Interchange*, 7 (1976-1977), 46-52.
3. GOODMAN, YETTA, and DOROTHY J. WATSON. "A Reading Program to Live With: Focus on Comprehension," *Language Arts*, 54 (December 1977), 868-879.

4. HALLIDAY, M.A.K. *Exploring the Functions of Language*. London: Edward Arnold, 1973.
5. MARECEK, MIRIAM. "Silver Sandals and Golden Tassels: Enriching Language Experiences for Young Children," *Language Arts*, 55 (January 1978), 30-40.
6. NORTON, DONNA E. "A Web of Interest," *Language Arts*, 54 (November/December 1977), 928-932.

Closer involvement and communication between the home
and school could become a most enjoyable, exciting, and
challenging area because most parents are quite interested
in learning how to teach their children.—Carl B.
Smith, *Parents and Reading*, 1971

Home Remedies for Reluctant Readers

John A. Childrey, Jr.
Florida Atlantic University

The purpose of the following groupings of ideas is to suggest to
parents and teachers alternative methods for involving
children and adolescents in the reading process. These
recommendations are based on the premise that reluctant
readers are able to read, but for some reason they choose not to
read. An additional premise is that positive intervention
activities are possible on the part of the parent. In fact, the
parent's role is crucial in establishing positive habits involving reading.

The tentative herb cures implicit in the title are only
suggestive of the vast array of gimmicks, tomfoolery, and
quackery which pass for home cures for reluctant readers.
What follows is a potpourri of notions, lye soap, foxfire,
overgeneralizations, garlic bags, and admonishments for
home use when teenage reluctant readers are suspected.

Some Admonitions and Suggestions

Any of the following suggested remedies may require
large amounts of time, comfort, love, care, patience, wisdom,
courage, discipline, rosemary, parsley, and sage. Trying a
remedy without a context and out of context may prove
injurious to your teen's reading health. However, thinking
about and exploring variations on a remedy may even be more
effective with a specific reader than following the suggestion
too literally.

Model Reading Behavior for Your Teen

The role of reading in the adult world is reflected by the parent. Beginning readers who see their parents read start out with more positive attitudes about reading. By teen years other influences compete in the developing value system. Teens are attempting to assert their individuality, yet parents are still among the most influential adult role models available. During this period in reluctant readers' lives, the reading that takes place in the home is important.

1. Have books in the home. Easy accessibility is the key. The books should be read and talked about. Records (or tapes) of books are available so that families can spend time listening together to a book they have read. Television has dramatized or made movie versions of books, offering a source of comparison. (How was the book like or different from the movie?) Books need to be reread. Books need to be bought, thus demonstrating the value placed on books by allocating money just as one might for food, clothing, shelter, and entertainment. A variety of books can be purchased: paperbacks, hardbacks, used books (which can be bought and resold), precious books, and expensive books. Books are available in bookstores, book clubs, drugstores, second hand thrift shops, and even garage sales.

2. Have newspapers in the home.

3. Provide periodicals (news magazines, special hobby or interest magazines for teens or children): *Cricket, Highlights, Boys Life, Jack and Jill, Ranger Rick, Mademoiselle* are just a few of those available.

4. Structure the family reading time. Have a reading hour. Set aside a reading space, a favorite chair or sofa or room. Encourage and allow your teen to read in the same room while you read.

5. Bargain for time. If the teen wants to spend an hour watching a television special, then the teen should spend an hour reading. The interaction gives both parent and teen a chance to talk. Make good bargains so that both bargainers "win."

6. Tell your teen how you learned to read. Tell stories of how famous people have been affected by books or reading.

7. Be natural about reading. If you don't like to read, but accept the need to influence your reluctant reader, then begin

with highly interesting material for yourself. Find other adults who do like to read and invite them to share with you what you might share with your reader. Ask your friends to invite you and your reader to participate in their reading hours. The sharing of opinions, interests, and tastes in reading can be very stimulating. Treat the sharing as a special occasion, a low-keyed celebration, perhaps with special food.

Read with Adolescents

1. Select a mutually attractive book—one a friend suggests, one of controversy, a classic, or one the teen thinks might be fun to read.

2. Read to the teen. Teens read so much on their own that for most it's a reward to have someone read to them.

3. Read in a comfortable position and manner. Trying to make the characters come alive is difficult even with training and practice. This is not to say "don't read with expression," but anything can be done.

4. Read for a comfortable length of time. Gradually increasing the time involvement will extend the listening attention of the reluctant teen participant. Begin with a portion of a chapter. Read the material ahead of time so you can make a good initial impression. Share the responsibility with your spouse or a friend.

5. See if friends would like to join the reading, first at your house, then at theirs. If this is too structured, alternate weeks or times. More than once a week seems preferable, but every day may be a little too much for interfamily sharing.

6. Call attention to community figures who read. Examples are newscasters; politicians; actors who read lines; television hosts who read via teleprompters; public readers at the library, and public lecturers or readers of poetry.

7. Much of the reading to teens will directly increase ability to listen. Listening can be strengthened by having teens respond after difficult words or concepts are read. "What do you think that means?" "Can you put that into your own words?" "Would you have acted like that given a similar situation?" "How do you think this will turn out?" "What will happen next?" "Why?"

8. "Why?" might be the most effective question to stimulate reasoning in a listening situation. The teen is called

on for evidence. The teen is responsible for evaluating the evidence and responding.

9. The sharing of reading—the time, the intimacy, the reactions (pro and con), the openness and attempt at dialogue—may be difficult to establish but may have a far reaching effect upon the attitude toward reading in a mutually beneficial manner.

10. Reading to the teen helps set a base for eventual discrimination of good writing from bad.

11. Orally read poetry, plays, and short stories with spouse and teens and friends. Begin with exciting plays with simple dialogue, try experimental things. Don't overdo the play or poem or short story however. Carrying a reading over for a night or two may stimulate the teen's interest.

12. Try not to strong arm reading in place of the normal activities in the day's events. Forcing a teen to give up peer activities may result in recalcitrance. However, in attempting an adult role model, it is important to set ground rules— "Reading will take place Monday-Thursday between dinner and dessert." "From 5:30-6 p.m. we will read the daily newspaper (the Bible, *Tom Sawyer*, or whatever)." Once scheduled, try to keep to the schedule. Space the time or vary it to prevent boredom or the feeling of drudgery.

Read Aloud

1. Set aside some time for the teen to read aloud to you. Reading to someone should instill confidence. Offer help with unfamiliar words.

   a. When reading for practice tell the teen the unknown word.

   b. Write down unfamiliar words.

   c. At the end of a paragraph or chapter, ask what the word meant and try to develop a sense of determining meaning from other clues in the reading.

   d. Ask the teen what the reading means. Ask him to listen to his own reading—at first, you may have to help—gradually have the teen take the responsibility for summarizing the reading.

   e. Praise the teen in adult terms for progress in gaining confidence, smooth flow of reading, or being able to retell what was read.

2. Have the teen read aloud homework, pleasurable or highly interesting material, and some required reading. Note the different purposes for reading with the teen. You don't read mathematics the way you read a sports magazine.

3. Have the teen read aloud cereal boxes, directions, maps, announcements. Here the teen must slow down and will see that each word is important.

4. Be a willing listener. Compare what you hear the teen reading with what is on the page.

5. Try to enjoy the teen's reading. At first, with a reluctant teen, this may be very difficult. By asking that a variety of things be read, you and the teen will be pleasantly surprised at unexpected findings of good and interesting reading.

Develop a Library Habit and Research Reading

Developing independence in reading skills is important for school achievement. Encouraging library use and helping students learn how to find information will aid in their reaching independence. Usually the reluctance barrier falls when the reader discovers an area of interest, a piece of information that is obscure or long forgotten. (Finding the name of a third greatgrandfather in a genealogical search is a marvelous reward for a child or teen.)

1. Enlist the aid of the school and local librarian. Ask them to provide you with current high interest reading. Often, being the first to read a book that later becomes popular will raise the esteem of the teen.

2. Set aside some time to explore the library with the teen. What are the rules? Where are the special shelves for fiction, nonfiction? What services are available? How can the reference librarian be of most help? What information do you need to have when you use various services of the library?

3. Set a regular visiting time for the library. Go with the teen and enjoy the time spent on this special event. Know the opening and closing hours. Walk or ride bicycles or public transportation. Know the joys and difficulties of "getting there." Teens are sometimes too shy to go places alone, or without a parent; sometimes inviting a friend along overcomes self-consciousness.

4. Know what media aids are available. Films and records or cassettes provide additional sources of stimulation for reading at the library.

5. Dig your "Roots." Reference and research are often tedious outside of a real task. So many records are available on interlibrary loan or microfilm that finding the family's genealogical lines can be fascinating and a genuine learning experience. The teen must use indexes, atlases, maps, and many other resources. In addition, background matter, social and political events, and architecture fill in gaps which census records cannot provide.

Develop research reading. In looking at the usefulness of library habits and the need for facts to solve controversies, the need for research reading is established.

6. Natural topics which need background information are prime targets for research: family trees, political decisions, or local environmental issues.

7. Artificial topics from school often reflect academic needs.

8. Self selected topics occur from interests.

Developing Reading from Interests

1. Talk to the teen about observed interests. Make a list of the various interests the teen has. The librarian can suggest reading matter suitable for finding out about interests.

2. Whenever practical, try to share some of the interests with the teen. While this may be difficult at a time when teen and parent seemingly have different interests, or the teen is trying out a multiplicity of options, the ability to talk about common knowledge and interests will bring the reading about interests into a conversation in a natural way.

3. Invest time and energy as well as some money in reasonable interests. Investing a large amount of money in an interest which wanes may be a source of friction; so, read about costs of equipment and talk about priorities of interests. How much money is needed? How much can the teen contribute? How much will the parent contribute (invest)? How long will interests last?

Establishing priorities is especially important, if and when the topic of owning and operating a car occurs. Most teens, it seems, are painfully unaware of maintenance, insurance, and repair costs, as well as the legal obligations associated with the purchase of an automobile. Parents often use this lack of information to postpone purchase, but it is a good learning and reading opportunity to get the facts prior to buying.

4. In general, interests provide a real reading experience for the teen. Vicarious experiences are almost as real as being there. Certainly one's reading experiences provide a chance to "try on" a new situation. How do others face primitive camping? What are the fears of a cliff diver, a hang glider, or a scuba diver? Conversely, what excitement is experienced?

5. Interest allow parents and teens the opportunity to read common sources and react to what is read and discovered. Discovering together both through reading and through activities diminishes reluctance.

Reading from Controversy

1. Don't be afraid to read together books which will likely develop friendly controversy with the teen. After all, it is in the mutual give and take, the fact finding, the examination of opinions that some measure of maturity will take place.

2. Taboo topics frighten most parents. How much should we assume the teen knows? How much do we know? It won't take long for all of us to find out if we read an article or book about sexual mores, running away from home, homosexual rights, pot smoking, or murder.

3. Political awareness probably ought to start at home. Why was the death penalty contested? Why should we abolish it? Why should we try to keep it? Often we need to read deeper, beyond the emotional issues, and find the facts. Having a teen around keeps parents honest and uncomfortable in evaluating another's opinion. Talking and reading through an issue may create temporary discord but can assist the critical reading of the teen. The reluctance to "prove" Mom and Dad wrong may disappear, mysteriously.

Developing a Vocabulary: Words from a Family Feud

The words children and teens use at home sometimes are not the words they need for success as a reader or in school achievement. Encouraging dictionary, thesaurus, and encyclopedia skills is difficult at best until the habit is firmly set. The following suggestions are found in many reading professional texts and journals and have been summarized here as suggestive of reinforcement activities as teens and children develop their vocabularies.

1. Vocabulary words are placed in a large box or can. The teen takes one word out and has five minutes or less to figure out what it means. Then each teen "describes" his word to the family and the family must try to guess his word.

2. Before reading a new story or book, pick out words the teen will have trouble with. Fold index cards and put one word on the outside of each card. Open the card and write what the teen is to do with the word (for example, write synonym or antonym, use in a sentence, etc.).

3. Ask teen to list as many prefixes and suffixes as he can and then allow him to check in a dictionary and add to the list. He should then search through a newspaper for ten words appropriate for combining with the suffixes and prefixes. New words will be formed by the teen and the meanings will be discussed.

4. Given a figure of speech in a sentence across the top of a paper, each teen will draw a literal interpretation of the sentence. At the bottom of the paper, the teen will rewrite the sentence in nonfigurative language.

5. Provide the teen with a passage to be read. Underline various words throughout the passage and, at the end, list less common words that can replace the underlined words and retain the meaning. The teen must choose the appropriate word from the list to match an underlined word.

6. During a set period, the teen can collect: the longest word, the current "in" or new slang words, the lingo of American sports such as football, or words that sound like what they mean (woosh). Found words can be displayed on bulletin boards.

7. To increase the vocabulary of the intermediate child, each day list four or five new words on the refrigerator. It is up to the teen to look up these words during the day. During the latter part of the day, the child will discuss the new words as definitions, as in context, and as of comprehensive points of view.

8. Have the teen choose an unusual word. Then for an activity, make a scrapbook of people, things, or places that deal with that word. Scrapbooks can be shared.

9. Play word games: Scrabble, Bingo, Spill and Spell, Jeopardy, Password, crossword puzzles.

10. Invite another family over to play "Family Feud." This is really a categorization game. So any kind of categorization will work: presidents, politicians, cars, books, etc.

Read for Fun and Practice

Many people accept the notion that one learns to read by reading. Once the skills of early reading are mastered, this notion seems sound. Everything that can be read probably is. At various points in a lifetime a reader eyes printed words everywhere. My mother tells me I learned by reading Donald Duck comics, not Dick and Spot and Jane and Sally as my teacher thought.

1. Comics are the dessert. Not desert, mind you, dessert. On Sunday, they're colorful; the rest of the time, pure fun.

2. Comics from the drug store are serious business. Many people learned to read by reading comic books.

In reading comics, the teen takes the pressure off. Usually there is no intrinsic value to the comic, but it serves a very useful value: reading is for fun. Some semiserious studies indicate that the vocabulary and readability levels of comics are higher than some high school textbook levels. The readability level of many comics is much higher than the tested reading level of some of the teens who read them. Are the teens using picture context clues? Are they looking at other teens read? What is happening? The reluctance to read comics is not usually present in the same teen who is reluctant to read. I suspect anxiety is missing because nobody really wants teens to read comics, so perhaps a "forbidden fruit" syndrome is occurring. I suspect that interest is playing a part. Since no functional literacy exam faces teens once they read the comics, they read.

3. The admonition for home remedy: let the teen read.

Understanding sports might fit more comfortably under a specialized interest. Sports enthusiasts among teens seem to far outnumber nonenthusiasts. Unfortunately, we often ignore some obvious ways to use this interest as a remedy for reluctance. Teens could read sports pages for sports news stories; sports magazines; sports biographies; sports novels, short stories, poems; sports encyclopedias; sports histories; sports periodicals; sports rules and regulations; sports monographs on "how to" perform, participate, be a good audience; and sports equipment catalogs.

If the available printed material on sports doesn't bend reluctant readers, they will probably become sports fallouts from expanded NFL coverage and will have to develop sports listening and viewing literacy.

Read everything: letters, diaries, journals, recipes, receipts, directions, memos, notes, homework, doodlings, grafitti, computer printouts, bills, statements of accounts, titles, contracts, insurance policies, movie tickets, record reveiws, *TV Guide*, teen magazines, weight reduction and record club ads, bank mortgage contracts, credit card applications and terms, credit sales interest terms, canned food and boxed food labels and ingredients, job want ads, driver's license instruction booklet, health pamphlets, IRS *Federal Income Tax Form* (long form), a reading textbook for teachers, special news articles, and billboards.

A formula is suggested that might apply to the reading of everything. Ten actions related to reading:

1. Read
2. React
3. Reread
4. Consider
5. Reflect
6. Evaluate
7. Share
8. Reflect
9. Reread
10. Conclude

Gift of Reading

This topic inadvertently suggests the seasonal gift giving of books. Books and magazine subscriptions are excellent holiday surprises. There is a difficulty—one which reflects the values of an older generation. Sometimes the recipient does not appreciate the gift. I encourage relatives to know the teen well before selecting books as gifts. Buying to an interest is preferable to buying from a reading teacher's recommended list; but, perhaps, a note with the gift of a book to indicate why the giver thought this particular title was chosen would help the teen receiving the book feel that thought and caring went into the selection.

Perhaps there is another gift of reading. I believe this is inherent in the desire of parents to want their teens to read "good" books—giving the teen some of the joy and excitement the adult felt as an adolescent or, perhaps, trying to prevent a distaste for reading held by the parent who recognizes that his own distaste is a barrier to shared enjoyment in reading.

In the April 9, 1978, "Hints from Heloise" column, still another kind of gift of reading was suggested: the thought of having an absent relative—in this instance, grandmother—record a story and send the taped story and book to the child for a read-along experience. With a teen, the gift of reading becomes a cherished visit with a grandparent or a separated parent. The chance for sharing an important part of one's value system is the gift of reading.

The Environment for Reading at Home

Up to this point the suggestions have implied an openness and acceptance of the teen's reluctance to read. The attitude of support on the part of the parent encourages or discourages the teen in overcoming that reluctance. The environment for reading is made up of many aspects:

1. Providing opportunities to read and react in an uncritical manner.
2. Systematic reflection of a critical reading opportunity.
3. Providing, even demanding, some shared experiences in reading.
4. Challenging, in a supportive manner, erroneous interpretations or conclusions not based on the reading. Jumping to conclusions, being swayed by loaded language, allowing emotions to persuade that logic can be dealt with without reflecting on the inferior judgment of the teen.

5. Showing, demonstrating to the teen a renewed emphasis on the value and the importance of reading in the adult world.

Creating a supportive home environment demands a certain relaxation of authority and an inclusion of some democratic self-direction on the part of the teen. The directive guidance for a reluctant reader may be the single hardest barrier to overcome. The impasse that may arise may require the counsel of a professional reading specialist. Teen reading, or inability to read, may become a source of friction; and parents and teen may have a difficult time coping.

Peer Reading

The teen who senses that Mom and Dad place importance on reading to satisfy themselves in adult life are more willing to take on this "adult" behavior than those who do not perceive their parents as readers. The presence in the home of books, newspapers, and magazines has long been acknowledged as a positive force in a teen's affective response to reading. Seeing peers read is important, so the parent should make certain that their teens have friends who read.

Several years ago, an adult student challenged me when I suggested providing teen friends who read. The response was the creation of a summer reading club. We called it the Teen Reading Club (TRC). For six weeks it attracted thirty teens three times a week from eleven to one o'clock. They read, worked in small groups, and heard from many adults concerning adult reading preferences or job related reading; a magician performed and suggested readings in magic and ESP; a novelist read portions of her latest book; poets read; a zoo keeper brought in a snake and a rodent and talked about pet care and suggested readings; library trips were taken; a local sportscaster talked about sports and mentioned his visit in his next report; and a TV announcer came in and talked about his experience as an actor in Hollywood and told how he "read" the news, the teletype service, and other essential print related activities which movie or TV audiences never see. A reading environment was created where teens saw other teens and adults reading and having their lives affected by reading.

Another teacher friend suggested bringing successful persons from the community to share the role of reading in the real world with vocational students. The positive response was staggering. Teens are not impressed with platitudes, but they are impressed with adults who honestly tell them what the role of reading *is* in adult life.

A Reflection

The teenager who reads will welcome every overture a parent makes. Well, almost; that teen is likely to be self-directing. Sometimes these reading teens will act as bridges to their nonreading counterparts. Most teens will respond positively if their parents' efforts to help are viewed as honest. For some teens a neutral third party is needed—an uncle, teacher friend, neighbor, retiree. In short, it may take a person to act as initial mediator to create a discussion that is reasonable and concerned with the problem and possible solutions.

Sometimes it will take a professional reading person to clearly delineate the goals for teacher, parent, and teen. When this happens, an honest effort should be made to consistently follow agreed upon guidelines to solve the reading problem of the teenager. The only possible way to solve a reading problem in the adolescent years is through a clear understanding of the difficulty and the commitment of all concerned to share in the effort to remediate. Teens must accept responsibility for learning (reading); Parents must commit support; teachers must provide the extent of the resources available.

All experiences that increase the child's aesthetic sensitivity to his environment will sharpen his perceptions and make it possible for him to express what he has noticed in some medium, be it art, music, or words.—Gertrude B. Corcoran, *Language Experience for Nursery and Kindergarten Years*, 1976

Motivating the Reluctant Reader through the Top Twenty

Cyrus F. Smith, Jr.
University of Wisconsin at Milwaukee

Carl Sandburg once defined poetry as "the capture of a picture, a song, or a flair, in a deliberate prism of words." Unfortunately, many adolescents never allow themselves an interface with this type of poetic experience. Similarly, many teachers consciously or subconsciously stifle poetic encounters within their classrooms. One way for a teacher to do this is to restrict students to the poetry found in prescribed anthologies. A second way is to restrict student reactions to deliberate prisons of words.

The intent of the author is to share some ideas which will give reluctant readers a chance to enjoy and experience poetry. Please note that this paper does not focus on the remedial reader but, rather, on the reluctant reader—the adolescent who can read but, typically, is reluctant to read. Poetry, especially of the kind found in school anthologies, is often rejected long before this person encounters it in the classroom. Needless to say, this attitude denies both the well intentioned, well prepared teacher and the skeptical, hostile student the satisfaction of a legitimate learning experience.

Lyrics Suitable for Teaching

Interestingly enough, reluctant readers often may be seen with transistor radios affixed to their heads. Upon closer inspection, one notes the students may be singing along with popular songs of the moment. The lyrics of these songs might provide the bases for poetry lessons. While not all verse found in popular music is suitable or appropriate for a teacher's consideration, from time to time an exceptional lyric appears. This author will consider lyrics of this sort as poetry suitable for teaching and the type of poetry that Sandburg may have had in mind when he further defined poetry as "... the report of a nuance between two moments when people say, 'Listen!' and 'Did you see it?' 'Did you hear it?' 'What was it?' "

As with most ideas in education, this one is by no means novel, unique, completely original, or unconditionally guaranteed. It is probably safe to say that most secondary language arts teachers have played records for their classes. As a student teacher, I can remember comparing "Richard Corry" by Edward Arlington Robinson to the recorded version of the poem by Paul Simon and Art Garfunkel. This proved to be an enjoyable experience for my students and myself. In fact, I initiated the nuance to which Sandburg alluded. Unfortunately, my lesson didn't completely continue within the guidelines he set forth. My follow-up activity compelled the students to write a paper comparing and contrasting the two versions of "Richard Corry." Their enjoyable experience now became punitive.

The Lesson Structure

This chapter is to consider a lesson structure which enhances the use of pop, folk, rock, or country lyrics in the language arts classroom. The lesson structure will more fully employ Sandburg's "nuance of the moment," in that students will not be confined to expressing themselves in traditional words. Specifically, we will explore alternative ways to explicate the poetry of popular songs. We will deviate from the traditional written explication to include the realms of listening, seeing, hearing, and feeling. The works of artists such as Jim Croce, John Hartford, Harry Chapin, Judy Collins, and John Denver can provide some usable classroom examples. This paper will focus on one song: "Vincent" by Don McLean.

"Vincent" is an exceptional example of modern lyric poetry presented in song format. The musical quality of the piece complements the hauntingly beautiful lyrics. When read at a literal level, the song relates the tragic story of a person named Vincent. In the course of the song, we learn that Vincent experiences rejection, suffering, and insanity. The combination of these elements culminates with Vincent's suicide.

Encouraging Creative Thinking

Teachers wishing to utilize this song for a visual explication will find it profitable to provide a copy of the lyrics fo each student. Have students read through the lyrics prior to listening to acquaint them with the intricacies of the verse as well as the high number of visual images. Students then can be directed to listen with a purpose, that is, to conjure up as many images as they can. Once this is done, the teacher should ask the students what visual images came to them during the listening session. It is important for the teacher to confine this discussion to the poem and not to allow students to ramble. The emphasis of this discussion should be on clarity, not ambiguity. If, in the discussion, the students have neglected to discuss an important image, the teacher needs to ferret this out. Open ended questions, designed to bring an obscure image into sharper focus, are most effective.

Alternative Explications

Once students have shared their personal visual perceptions, the teacher should begin in earnest to prepare students for the alternative explication. It is important here for students to decide who Vincent is. One possible suggestion is that Vincent is a friend or acquaintance of the poet. However, if students are assigned to scan the lyrics looking for words and terms with some common bond, many "art" and "art related" items appear. For example, *pallet, paint, sketch, hue,* and *artist* are used with regular frequency. As students scan the lyrics, the teacher writes on the chalkboard the headings "art" and "art related." The teacher then categorizes the students' vocabulary contributions under the appropriate heading *only* if students can justify the inclusion of their particular word(s). With some words, it may be necessary for student volunteers to consult the dictionary for a specific "art" usage. Coincidentally, this is also a good time for the teacher to subtly incorporate vocabulary skills teaching through structural analysis and context clues.

When the vocabulary search is completed, there will be enough documented evidence to propose that the Vincent of the song is an artist. In fact, some students may wish to suggest that Vincent is Vincent Van Gogh. However, more evidence is needed before this assumption can be affirmed or denied.

The research for the evidence initiates a significant event in the alternative explication of the song. This research can be done in the classroom provided the necessary resources are made available. These resources are in the form of portfolios, collections, and museum catalogs of Van Gogh prints. Such books as Robert Wallace's *The World of Van Gogh, 1850-1890* and Meyer Schapiro's *Vincent Van Gogh* are excellent resources. By searching through books such as these (others are listed in the bibliography of this paper), students, either individually or in small groups, will find evidence to corroborate many of the Van Gogh inferences found in the lyrics. Further, many of the vague and obscure lines, as well as some rather obvious ones, will suddenly sharpen within this context. For instance, the phrase "starry, starry night" is repeated four times within the song. Coincidentally, this phrase is the title of two Van Gogh paintings. One of these was painted in September 1888, the other in June 1889. Further, the painting "Road with Cypresses" dated May 1890 depicts a brilliantly illuminated night sky. The line "Catch the breeze and the winter chills" can be seen in the painting "Road in the Snow at Etten," 1881. The Lyric, "Flaming flowers that brightly blaze," is brought to life in at least two of Van Gogh's paintings. For instance, "Flowers" (no date) and "Sun-flowers," August 1888, both could be used to visually explicate this line. The landscapes entitled, "Harvesting Wheat in the Alpelles Plain," June 1888, "Green Corn," 1889, and "Field of Spring Wheat at Sunrise," March 1890 could be used to visually document the lines "Look out on a summer's day" or "Moving fields of amber grain." In fact, at least 28 specific works of Van Gogh's art can be referenced to the lyrics of "Vincent." (A list of Van Gogh's paintings that coincide with "Vincent" can be found at the end of this chapter.)

Once this supporting evidence has been collected, students should be presented with an alternative way to interpret "Vincent." One very effective way would be to have students create an audiovisual program which synchronizes slide reproductions of Van Gogh's paintings with McLean's music and lyrics. Students would be responsible for all facets of this production. They would begin by selecting appropriate Van Gogh prints from the sources listed earlier and those included in the reference section of this chapter. Next, students would make slides of the chosen prints. This is easily done with an Instamatic camera and either a 3 x 3 (for smaller prints) or an 8 x 8 (for larger prints) camera stand. If the school does not have this equipment available, it can be rented from a photographic supply store for about $10. The cost of film, development, and mounting for 40 slides would normally run about $8. Once the slides have been developed and mounted, the students would synchronize the slides and music, using a carousel slide projector and either a tape recorder, cassette recorder, or a record player. More elaborate productions employ dissolve units, allowing two or more slide projectors to operate simultaneously. Finally, students would compare and contrast their group productions by showing them to one another. The expense of this venture, while minimal, can be defrayed by exploring the audiovisual resources available within the school. Some schools and most school systems have the necessary equipment as well as the facilities for developing and mounting slides.

Emphasis on Reading

It should be pointed out that reading is the focus of a project such as this. Students must first read the long lyrics for primary meaning. This work at the literal level is enhanced by vocabulary skills teaching. Second, students begin to explore a variety of possible interpretations with the teacher's guidance. This second stage involves such higher thinking skills as comparison and contrast, anticipation, sequencing, inference, application, and evaluation. Students then apply these components in a stimulating and motivating experience.

While teachers are cordially invited to have their students create their own explications of "Vincent," you may also wish to challenge your students with similar projects. One such project would be to have them read the lyrics to the song, "American Pie," also by Don McLean.* Have them focus on the lines which read:

A long, long time ago,
I can still remember
How that music use't to make me smile.
And, I knew if I had my chance
That I could make those people dance
And maybe they'd be happy for awhile.
But, February made me shiver
With every paper I'd deliver.
Bad news on the doorstep!
I couldn't take one more step.
I can't remember if I cried
When I read about his widowed bride
But, something touched me deep inside
The day the music died.

Then, give the students the following information:

Charles Hardin Holley assumed the stage name of Buddy Holly in the mid 1950s. He recorded such early rock and roll hits as "Handy Man" and "Peggy Sue." On August 15, 1958 he married Marie Santiago. On February 3, 1959, Holly boarded a private airplane with fellow performers Richie Valens and J.P. "The Big Bopper" Richardson. The plane crashed upon takeoff in Clear Lake, Iowa.

Using this information and the opening lyrics of "American Pie," have students begin to trace the history of rock and roll from 1959 to 1972. It is important that they see the coincidence between the phrases "widowed bride," "February made me shiver," "Bad news on the doorstep," and the biographical information about Buddy Holly. Next, initiate a discussion which asks the students to contribute the names of individuals, titles of famous rock groups, and significant events associated with this time period. Make sure this list includes the following musicians, political figures, and events: Bob Dylan, Jimi Hendrix, Janis Joplin, Elvis Presley, The Birds, The Beatles, The Rolling Stones, The Supremes, Robert Kennedy, Martin Luther King, Jr., John F. Kennedy, the

Vietnam War, the Woodstock Rock Festival, and the student protests of the middle to late '60s. Students now should be directed to reread the lyrics associating these people, places, and events within the context of the song.

One alternative explication for "American Pie" would be for students to produce a slide-tape program. This project would follow guidelines similar to the "Vincent" lesson described earlier, but would utilize album covers and pictures of events alluded to in the song. A second alternative for an explication of "American Pie" would be to have students compare and contrast an original Buddy Holly hit, "Handy Man," to the later release by James Taylor.

Another alternative explication that teachers might try would be to visually compare Alfred Lord Tennyson's poem, "The Eagle," to John Denver's song, "The Eagle and the Hawk." Finally, "Song for Duke" by Judy Collins and "Sir Duke" by Stevie Wonder provide material for a lesson of comparison and contrast. Both songs can be compared as tributes to the late Duke Ellington. However, the lyrics and music of each provide interesting contrasts in both style and treatment of the same theme.

Summary

Some of the music that is popular with adolescents may be used by teachers to motivate reluctant readers. Teachers will find that the lyrics of many songs provide excellent sources for teaching vocabulary development and both literal and higher levels of comprehension. Since the lyrics of many songs will affect students in many different ways, the teacher must be careful not to lose sight of lesson objectives within the forest of "alternative" explications. The necessary factor, then, is the teacher. The teacher must be flexible enough to encourage creative thinking and artistic expression but, at the same time, confine student reactions within reasonable boundaries of the song in question. Students who cannot legitimately support an alternative explication should not be allowed to continue until substantiation can be provided.

While this paper has explored poetic explications which deviate from a traditional written model, teachers should realize that not every lyric will lend itself to an audiovisual

Smith

interpretation. However, the lyrics of numerous songs can be used as the nucleus of an effective reading related lesson. For instance, students can be directed to scan a lyric to find nouns, verbs, adjectives, or adverbs. Or other lyrics might be perused for examples of more sophisticated literary devices such as metaphor, simile, oxymoron, and personification. Whatever form a lesson of this sort takes, it must be controlled by the teacher.

The intent of this paper is to get reluctant readers to read. If the teacher is unsure of the lesson objectives or fails to establish reasonable working parameters, the lesson could deteriorate into little more than a listening session. Therefore, in order to capitalize on the popularity of contemporary music for in-class use, teachers must be aware of their roles and responsibilities. Then, the lyrics of pop, folk, rock, or country musicians will not only mirror social values but also will become springboards to recreational reading.

Van Gogh Paintings Which Can Be Used to Illustrate the Song "Vincent" by Don McLean

Starry Night, 1889.
Portrait of Vincent Van Gogh, Paris, 1887, painted by Toulouse-Lautrec.
The Sower, June 1888.
Self-Portrait, undated.
Wheat Field with Reaper, 1889.
Undergrowth, 1890.
Rain Effect, undated.
Skull with Cigarette, January 1886.
Flowers in a Copper Vase, undated.
Landscape with Cypresses, 1889.
Self-Portrait, Paris, 1887.
Wheat Fields with Crows, Auvers, July 1890.
The Harvest, June 1888.
Self-Portrait with Straw Hat and Pipe, 1887.
Old Peasant (Patience Escalier), Arles, August 1888.
Peasant Woman, Brabant Headdress, 1885.
The Potato Eaters, April-May 1885.
The Night Cafe, September 1888.
Portrait of the Artist, Saint Remy, September 1889.
Self-Portrait with Pipe and Bandaged Ear, Arles, February 1889.
Portrait of Dr. Gachet, Auvers, June 1890.
The Postman, Roulin, August 1888.
Portrait of Lieutenant Milliet, September 1888.
On the Way to Work, undated.
The Sower, 1888.
Self-Portrait with Straw Hat, undated.

Self-Portrait, Paris, January-February 1888.
Self-Portrait, undated.
Self-Portrait with Gray Hat, Paris, September-December 1887.
Self-Portrait, Saint Remy or Auvers, late 1889-1890.

References

BOOKS

SALINGER, MARGARETTA M. *The Metropolitan Museum of Art: Vincent Van Gogh.* New York: Book of the Month Club, 1952.

SANDBURG, CARL. *The Complete Poems of Carl Sandburg: Revised and Expanded Edition.* New York: Harcourt Brace Jovanovich, 1969, 317, 319.

SCHAPIRO, MEYER. *Vincent Van Gogh.* New York: Harry N. Abrams.

Van Gogh: Paintings and Drawings. Montreal, Quebec: Montreal Museum of Fine Arts Catalogue, 1960.

Vincent Van Gogh: Paintings and Drawings. San Francisco: M. H. DeYoung Memorial Museum Catalogue, 1958.

Vincent Van Gogh (1853-1890). Baltimore: Baltimore Museum of Art Catalogue, 1970.

WALLACE, ROBERT. *The World of Van Gogh, 1853-1890.* New York: Time-Life Books, 1969.

RECORDS

"American Pie" from the album *American Pie* by Don McLean. United Artists Records, Inc.

"Sir Duke" from the album *Songs in the Key of Life* by Stevie Wonder. Motown Records, Inc.

"Song for Duke" from the album *Judith* by Judy Collins. The Wild Flower Company. (ASCAP), Electra/Asylum/Nonesuch Records.

"The Eagle and the Hawk" from the album *John Denver's Greatest Hits* by John Denver. RCA Records, Inc.

"Vincent" from the album *American Pie* by Don McLean. United Artists Records, Inc.

Avoid the series books such as the Nancy Drew or Hardy
Boys series. They're so similar that if a child reads one the
next one doesn't require any effort.—Virginia Haviland,
Library of Congress, 1977

Recent Adolescent Literature:
An Alternative to the Serials

Alfred J. Ciani
University of Cincinnati

It seems that many issues dealing with education exist on a
pendulum basis. That is, public sentiment shifts from one
extreme to another. In the early part of this century, reading
was almost totally an oral activity and it was only through the
efforts of Buswell (3) and Judd and Buswell (8) that the
emphasis shifted from oral to silent reading and to reading for
different purposes with a variety of materials. Russell cited an
attempt by Agnew (1) to objectively consider the advantages
and disadvantages of phonics instruction. Forty years later
this debate still occurs. More recently, the back to basics and
minimum competency standards issues seem to be of great
importance to educators and to the public.

Probably due to "good old days" sentiments and some
television programing, there seems to be a rebirth in the
popularity of serial fiction of the Bobbsey, Drew, and Hardy
genre.

Why Not?

Beckman (2), of the University of Waterloo, flatly states
that serials such as the Bobbsey Twins should not be in any
school library. Many public children's librarians hold similar
views (5). Beckman facetiously poses the question, "Why not
the Bobbsey Twins?" and provides three reasons—the first
being cost. It seems there is never enough money to purchase

all the books teachers recommend or that librarians would like to shelve. Entwined with the question of cost is judgment or the actual selection of books. Teachers and librarians typically are exposed to evaluation criteria while in training. Huck (6) refers to key elements (plot, setting, theme, characterization, style, format) that are often of poor quality in the serials genre. Typically, the plot in these books is developed by a single person and then fleshed out by ghost-writers. Faced with smaller budgets for new acquisitions, teachers and librarians seek only those books which rate high in the key elements of literature.

Time is a second reason for rejecting or limiting the purchase of the serial novels. There are only a few years in which adolescents can read for pleasure as adolescents. These books can certainly be read later on when adolescents become adults, but books for adolescents are so much more meaningful if read while in that particular age bracket.

The effect of mediocrity is the third reason for rejection of this genre. Ginsburg (4) states that the basic pattern of these series remains unchanged. For instance, in the Drew series, each episode begins with a mysterious event, followed by a menacing phone call, message, or visit. Proceeding undaunted, Nancy frequently receives a bump on the head (at last count over thirty), is captured, then escapes and quickly solves the mystery. Perhaps some readers find comfort or escape in formula fiction. However, it seems that a common goal of all teachers is to enable students to stretch their minds and let them grow.

Huck (6) maintains that when evaluating plot, it must be original and credible. Certainly, plots which are outlined by one author, hacked out by another, with dialogue possibly added by a third—all conforming to the structure of a series— are at least repetitive. The awareness of key elements of literature will enable the reader to avoid complacent acceptance which the series genre emulates.

The biased nature of the series books must not be tolerated in our society. For instance, the Bobbsey, Hardy, and Drew series have included an assortment of minor black characters portrayed as maids, porters, or cooks. Furthermore, Jones (7) states that the Drew villains were often from a racial or minority group and although the authors maintain that

Nancy never jumped to conclusions, she constantly indulged in first impressions. It is true that the Bobbsey books contained prominent black characters. However, these characters, Dinah and Sam, retained the racist image of shuffling, good natured servants with wide grins—all variations of the Sambo theme. Although the serials are being revised, the Council on Interracial Books for Children maintains that racism cannot be edited out of books for students (9). In the Bobbsey serials, Dinah and Sam remain loyal and contented servants whose superstitious natures, emotionalism, and physical traits provide the major comic ingredients.

What Are Some Alternatives

The age old question arises: Should we provide what is good or what entertains? It seems honest to advocate both positions. Do almost anything that will get any reader into a book. Then, teachers or librarians, functioning as guides, can expose students to evaluation criteria and show them how they can establish their own preferences. With a suggested book list, where students may make choices about what to read, the essence of the notions of what is good and what entertains will naturally emerge.

The next step is to locate recently published adolescent literature. The following annotated bibliography should help teachers select new titles to share with students. Any list will reflect the bias of the reviewer. This list should be considered as a starter and by no means the best of what all students might read but, hopefully, there will be a few titles which will appeal to some students.

Contemporary Fiction

The most interesting aspect of the books in this genre is how well teenagers relate to each other. The honesty in their relationships is a welcome addition and will certainly help in nurturing the minds of a future generation.

Samuels, G. *Adam's Daughter*. New York: Thomas Y. Crowell, 1977, 209 pp., $6.95.
Robert Adam was sent to prison for killing a man. His daughter Robyn had not seen him for six years. Although forbidden

to meet with him after his parole, Robyn does and begins to form a very special relationship with her real father. Through sharing the frustrations and hostilities her father experiences, Robyn develops a keen insight.

Jones, A. *The Hawks of Chelney.* New York: Harper and Row, 1978, 245 pp., $7.95.

Honesty is one aspect teachers would like reinforced. Siri and Thea develop an honest relationship. Siri loves the wild beauty of the hawks. He is forced to hide among the cliffs when local villagers' superstitions cause them to suspect that the boy and the hawks have something to do with the poor fish catch. Thea changes his life and they become involved in a mysterious twist of fate.

Ferry, C. *O Zebron Falls!* Boston: Houghton Mifflin, 1977, 213 pp., $7.95.

Teenagers in any time or setting seem to experience the same frustrations. Zebron Falls, Michigan, is the setting for this novel with a backdrop of World War II. Lukie Bishop experiences the fairly typical joys and disappointments of most teenagers. Yet the special circumstance of a World War adds interesting complications. All comes to a rather special moment at the high school graduation.

Kerr, M.E. *Gentlehands.* New York: Harper and Row, 1978, 183 pp., $6.95.

Honest relationships make for strong plots. Skye Pennington of New York City and of Beauregard (a spacious summer home in Sayville, New York) and Buddy Boyle, a full-time resident of Sayville, developed such a relationship. Seemingly from two different worlds, these teenagers fall in love. Yet a dark secret about to unravel concerning Buddy's grandpa would soon send their relationship churning.

Peck, R. *Are You in the House Alone?* New York: Dell, 1977, 172 pp., $1.25.

Gail, a high school junior, begins to receive strange, weird, and even psychotic messages from an unknown person. When she seeks help, the female counselor in her high school initially accuses her of a fantasy. After the rape, the police treat her as if she were the criminal. The theme is quite popular in the movies and television. Although written for ages fourteen and up, the book is also popular with middle school students.

Kerr, M.E. *Dinky Hocker Shoots Smack.* New York: Dell, 1972, 190 pp., $.95.

You can always tell when students enjoy a book. They may not tell the teacher, but careful observation will detect when a book is liked. Dinky and her friend Tucker are honest with each other. They are faced with problems and deal with them mutually. A funny and often pointed story of how lonely a teenager can be while "growing up."

Mazer, N.F. *Dear Bill, Remember Me?* New York: Dell, 1976, 195 pp., $1.50.
A collection of eight short stories that will appeal to all teenager girls. The stories are delicate yet reveal a clear understanding of the ambitions, anxieties, and neat happenings in the lives of teenage girls.

Wersba, B. *Tunes for a Small Harmonica.* New York: Dell, 1976, 175 pp., $1.25.
At age twelve, J.F. (for Jacqueline Frances) decides to evermore dress in men's clothes. At age sixteen, J.F. falls in love with her poetry teacher. In an attempt to earn money for a favorite cause, she takes to the streets with her harmonica. In a simple way, she crusades for people and finds out about herself.

Science Fiction

Most of the books reviewed are collections of mysteries, including ghosts, vampires, and tales of the supernatural in commonplace settings. The short stories are especially appropriate for oral reading, a technique often neglected in the middle and senior high grades.

Le Guin, U.K. *Orsinian Tales.* New York: Bantam Books, 1977, 209 pp., $1.95.
Ursula Le Guin is an award winning science fiction writer. Her knack of relating feelings as if the reader were a participant in the story makes her stories credible. *Orsinian Tales* is a collection of eleven stories, all of which reflect a filigree-like intricacy and balance of the possible and probable.

Roach, M.K. *Encounters with the Invisible World.* New York: Thomas Y. Crowell, 1977, 131 pp., $6.95.
A fine collection of ten short tales. The collection of notes at the end of the book makes these tales intriguing. The author, a native of Massachusetts, has collected these stories from oral legend and archives from all over New England. She has not merely carried on the legends but has embellished them as only a good storyteller can and should.

Elwood, R. (Editor). *The 50-Meter Monsters and other Horrors: Six Tales of Terror.* New York: Pocket Books, 134 pp., 1976.
As the editor attests, this book is a collection of grotesque oddities. It includes thirsty vampires, terrifying monsters, and tales of the deep sea. All are just right to be read one at a time, right before going to sleep...if you can!

Wright, G. *Masters of Magic.* New York: Pyramid Books, 1976, 157 pp., $1.50.
If you are at least one bit curious about magic and how tricks are performed, this is the book for you. Magic secrets from

ancient times to the present are exposed—how people are sawed in half, how cars disappear, how to read minds, and all beneath the proscenium arch. The magic of the popular Amazing Kreskin, Doug Henning, and Uri Geller is related in these pages. An absolute must for every shelf.

Peck, R. *Ghosts I Have Been*. New York: Viking Press, 1977, 214 pp., $7.95.

Few writers can bring off the serious side of situations while allowing the lighter side its due. Peck has the ability to treat the haunting tragedy of this tale while the quiet humor takes its course. This is the tale of Blossom who, after stumbling on her gift of second sight, develops a mature outlook about her ability.

Pearce, P. *The Shadow Cage*. New York: Thomas Y. Crowell, 1977, 152 pp., $7.50.

Some collections of the supernatural are traditional in the sense that they are variations on the themes of vampires, headless riders, or clanging chained lepers. This is a collection of ten tales, all original. A refreshing look at eerie tales, including the best of chilling surprises and warnings of the future.

Sports

It seems that interest in sports has created a large and healthy audience. Recent titles include books about soccer, ocean racing, and cross country running. Of course, the most popular category is sports biographies and I have included four new titles.

Libby, B. *Thurmon Munson: Pressure Player*. New York: G.P. Putnam's Sons, 1978, 192 pp., $5.95.

Relates the story of a short and stocky farm boy who doesn't look like an athlete. However, this Ohio native who became a legend in high school athletics is compared to the all time great baseball catchers. He has batted five seasons with over a .300 average. He has caught in over 140 games for six years straight. After winning the World Series against the Dodgers, this Yankee great said that he would play the same whether he had 20 cents or $2 million in the bank, and the book helps you to believe him.

Burchard, M. *Sports Hero: Rod Carew*. New York: G.P. Putnam's Sons, 1978, $5.49.

An interesting aspect of sports biographies is the informal views provided the reader. Once out of his baseball uniform, Carew becomes one of the nicest persons in sports. He won the 1977 Roberto Clemente Citizenship Award for service to his community and adores his family. On the field, he once fined himself for not trying hard enough. Reggie Jackson refers to him as an artist with a bat. Large print makes this an excellent title for reluctant readers.

Tuttle, A. *Steve Cauthen: Boy Jockey.* New York: G. P. Putnam's Sons, 1978, 47 pp., $7.95.

What makes this book a winner is the simple yet informative story of a young man's success. When he began at just sixteen years of age, Cauthen faced typical frustrations of most young people. There are many adolescents capable of relating to Steve Cauthen. The large pictures make this an excellent book for any collection. The only reservation is that the book was published just prior to his Triple Crown victory.

Lipsyte, R. *Free to Be Muhammad Ali.* New York: Harper and Row, 1978, 124 pp., $5.95.

What really adds a nice touch to this impressive story is the Epilogue in which Ali states, "I don't believe all the stuff I say." Included are reminiscences of the 1960 Olympic Games in Rome when Ali was eighteen years old. The action and posed photographs are a strong asset to the text.

Burchard, P. *Ocean Race: A Sea Venture.* New York: G.P. Putnam's Sons, 1978, 128 pp., $7.95.

An excellent book about sailing which makes no assumptions about previous experience with sailing. This book, with many pictures and a helpful glossary, is the story of a race from New England to Bermuda. Interest in this sport is growing and the book should be on all library shelves.

Stumbler, I. *Top Fuelers: Drag Racing Royalty.* New York: G.P. Putnam's Sons, 1978, 125 pp., $5.89.

This book reviews the merits of famous drag racers. The science of racing becomes evident as Big Daddy Don Garlits discusses his six factors for winning races. Many photographs and easy reading make this a must for every middle, junior, and senior high school library.

Jackson, C.P. *How to Play Better Soccer.* New York: Thomas Y. Crowell, 1978, 147 pp., $6.95.

Soccer is one of the most rapidly growing sports. On one summer afternoon in East Rutherford, New Jersey, the Cosmos soccer team drew over 72,000 spectators. This book discusses the popularity in foreign countries as well as the history of the game dating back to 1175 in England where it was outlawed for interfering with archery practice. The heart of the book is technique and the clear illustrations by Don Madden help to make the text easily understandable.

Knudson, R.R. *Fox Running.* New York: Avon Paperbacks, 1975, 126 pp., $1.25.

The author actually trained with the University of Arizona

track team in 1974 to understand the vigors of long distance running. This insight contributes to the development of a wonderful story of an Indian girl who helps others to understand life and to appreciate the world around them. A must for all to read.

Nonfiction

Included are two nonsport biographies for high school students. In addition, the titles in this section include a documentary information type book about the American Indian.

Nabokov, P. (Editor). *Native American Testimony*. New York: Thomas Y. Crowell, 1978, 242 pp., $8.95.
It is very difficult to understand what peace the white settlers found in their westward expansion. *Old Jules*, a book by Maria Sandoz, is the story of the settling of Nebraska. Sandoz recalls how her father struggled to tame the wilderness and tells of people freezing to death, going crazy in howling blizzards, and dying of disease and starvation. This book is a bittersweet account of the relationship between the "yellow eyes" and the native American Indians, how much the Indians loved the open prairie and sky, and how adept they were in survival. To any reader who has enjoyed *Bury My Heart at Wounded Knee* or *Black Elk Speaks* or *Custer Died for Your Sins*, this book is a must. This collection of documents is well worth reading and sharing.

The Impact Team. *The Weather Conspiracy*. New York: Ballatine Books, 1977, 234 pp., $1.95.
This is one of the most fascinating books you will ever read about the coming of a new ice age. The book is loaded with expert testimony and empirical investigations as well as two Central Intelligence Agency reports. The logical framework which is woven with these sources leads to an almost unthinkable conclusion. The question is not what if an ice age arrives, but how soon will the next ice age arrive?

Taylor, L.B. *Gifts from Space*. New York: John Day, 1977, 130 pp., $7.95.
At first thought, space seems empty, void of almost anything of value. However, the payoff comes as a byproduct of space exploration. That is, new medical techniques practiced with the astronauts can now be implemented commercially on earth. New energy ideas, weather tracking, environmental precautions, and a technical clearinghouse are available, thanks to our outer space explorations. This book is filled with accurate information for all.

Lisca, P. *John Steinbeck: Nature and Myth.* New York: Thomas Y. Crowell, 1978, 245 pp., $7.95.
Each person is unique. Biographers are those who try to relate not only the essence of individuals but their entire character. Lisca has succeeded in bringing together a diverse character for the reader. The twenty-five year experience of writing about Steinbeck is clearly apparent in this fine biography.

Devaney, J. *Hitler: Mad Dictator of World War II.* New York: G.P. Putnam's Sons, 1978, 222 pp., $7.95.
As the title implies, this nonfiction account of atrocities should not be ignored. A rather vivid account of Hitler. Devaney describes him in three aspects. The first of pallor, lost in a dream; the second as colorful, a stormy face, that of a lunatic; the third as a naive, dull, and rustic farmhand. I believe this biography is one which all students should read, lest we forget.

It is hoped that the books reviewed here will help teachers, librarians, and parents advise adolescents as to which books are recent and of better quality than the serial genre; that interest has been aroused and some of these books will soon appear in the hands of readers, whether they be adolescents or adults; and that this list will be passed along for others to peruse.

References

1. AGNEW, D.C. "The Effect of Varied Accounts of Phonetic Drill on Primary Reading," in D. Russell, "Reading Research that Makes a Difference," *Elementary English*, 38 (Fall 1961), 74-78.
2. BECKMAN, M. "Why Not the Bobbsey Twins?" *Ontario Library Review*, November 15, 1964.
3. BUSWELL, G.T. "An Experimental Study of the Eye-Voice Span in Reading," *Supplementary Educational Monographs*, No. 17, University of Chicago, 1920.
4. GINSBURG, J. "And Then There is Good Old Nancy Drew," *Ms.*, Volume 2, Number 7 (January 1974), 93-94.
5. HARRIS, C. Personal communication. Children's Room, Public Library of Cincinnati and Hamilton County, October 1977.
6. HUCK, C. *Children's Literature*, Third Edition. New York: Holt, Rinehart and Winston, 1976.
7. JONES, J. "Negro Stereotypes in Children's Literature: The Case of Nancy Drew," *Journal of Popular Culture*, Volume 1, Number 4 (Spring 1973).
8. JUDD, C.H., and G.T. BUSWELL, "Silent Reading: A Study of Various Types," Supplementary Educational Monographs, University of Chicago Press, 1922.
9. STARK, M.K. "Bert and Nan and Flossie and Fred: The Bobbsey Twins Roll On," *Bulletin*, Volume 6, Number 1 (1975). New York: Interracial Books for Children.

It is my firm belief that books for children can and must become an integral part of the total school curriculum, weaving in and out of every subject area.—Lee Bennett Hopkins, 1980

Motivating Adolescent Readers via Starter Shelves in Content Area Classes

David M. Bishop
Northern Kentucky University

Introduction

This discussion concerns a procedure for stimulating greater voluntary reading in secondary school content areas. The procedure focuses on the establishment and use of a high-interest "starter shelf" of paperback books related to the subjects taught in each content area classroom. Suggestions are offered for selecting material for a classroom starter shelf; initiating the use of a starter shelf; capitalizing on student interest in starter shelves; and keeping abreast of new, appropriate books. While emphasis is placed on increasing the reading of paperbacks under noninstructional conditions, some concluding comments indicate ways that teachers may more directly capitalize on the starter shelf in classroom discussions and assignments.

Current Views of Content Area Reading

Secondary and content area reading have received increased attention during the past ten years. The publication of Robinson and Thomas' *Fusing Reading Skills and Content* (40) and Herber's *Teaching Reading in Content Areas* (29) seems to have stimulated a reexamination of this important aspect of reading development. Today, a large number of new and revised texts concerning the adolescent reader and secondary programs (14, 30, 31, 41, 44,) are available, and frequent articles in journals such as *English Journal* and the *Journal of Reading* continue to add to our understanding. However, many unresolved issues are apparent. While it is impossible to explore all of these issues here, two are particularly important to the focus of this paper: 1) disagreement over the degree of involvement of content teachers in developing reading ability, and 2) the role of content teachers in encouraging lifetime reading habits of secondary school students.

Regarding the development of reading ability, many educators feel that the slogan "every teacher a teacher of reading" means placing heavier emphasis on all aspects of the traditional concerns of developmental reading appropriate for older readers; thus reading development becomes the curriculum, and the material read is of secondary importance. Others subscribe to an approach that emphasizes the goals of content learning first, with the guidance of textbook learning-through-reading a secondary (albeit important) consideration dependent upon student abilities and the reading/study skills needed for success in given course work. Peters (*36*) articulated an intermediate position, suggesting as a pragmatic matter that content teachers take on more (but not all) of the objectives of developmental reading since, as a group, they have a great amount of contact with students and since comprehensive reading programs and reading specialists are rarely available on a schoolwide basis in grades seven through twelve. The position taken here is that the degree and nature of content teacher involvement in developing reading ability depend on too many factors (needs of the district in general, group and individual student needs, monetary considerations, major objectives of content area classes, and content teacher knowledge of reading theory and practice) for a blanket statement to be appropriate in all situations. However, the starter shelf requires little money, time, or specific training for implementation and, as it can be used with students in varying ways, it should be adaptable to a number of different philosophies and settings.

The second issue, that of developing lifetime readers, encompasses a similar range of opinions. Many textbooks give adequate attention to affective developing in reading. However, English departments have traditionally shouldered much of the burden for expanding student interests in reading; changing attitudes toward reading; and developing a value structure wherein reading is willingly chosen as a worthwhile activity for purposes of recreation, escape, information gain, or aesthetic experience. Reading development in other content areas, on the other hand, has traditionally been viewed as academic/functional reading. Recent textbooks (41, 44) have provided some leads for integrating affective objectives in reading with content area concerns, and most such treatments depend on a considerable investment of time in planning and curricular adjustment to ensure success. The procedure described in this paper is designed for teachers who have not yet found the means for implementing extensive change and for those who, for reasons of philosophy and curricular design, do not wish to effect the broad shifts in emphasis detailed elsewhere.

Rationale for the Starter Shelf

There are several reasons for using classroom libraries of the type described here. The first is an availability factor. During the period when such researchers as Gray (23, 24) and Waples, Berelson, and Bradshaw (51) were investigating the factors influencing adult reading habits, the *lack* of appropriate material was often cited as a factor limiting reading. In contrast, today there are so many potentially interesting and rewarding reading materials available for adolescent readers that the array can be overwhelming. This availability of a wide range of reading matter in school libraries, public libraries, and bookstores can be an inhibiting factor, with students needing to know pretty well what they're after in order to find something they like. Book jacket illustrations and blurbs (which often emphasize the sensational) can be more misleading than informative and can further confuse or disappoint students looking for appropriate books. A smaller library on more limited topics within each content area classroom provides more focus for the student. Furthermore, some studies show that classroom libraries, when appropriately used to augment school libraries, increase students' voluntary reading (42).

Second, content area teachers get to know their students' interests and attitudes toward the content area. The content teacher is available for informal suggestions to students with particular needs and interests. Closely tied to this point is the likelihood that content teachers will be (or can more easily become) better versed on books available in their field and better judges of the quality of the content and interest levels of these books than other school personnel. While the school librarian may have a broad background of knowledge of many books, and the English teacher may be actively involved in the development of personal lifetime reading habits, neither can be equally well-informed in all of the possibilities open to students for satisfying reading needs. Thus, each content teacher can be a vital link between knowledge of student interests and knowledge of appropriate resources.

Third, the chances of reaching a student through personal contact are greatly enhanced if each content teacher has a starter shelf. Students often develop special relationships with one teacher because of personal factors or interest in a subject. Students who develop these relationships may accept or even seek out suggestions on reading from a favorite teacher while other teachers' efforts go unappreciated.

Fourth, in seeing a variety of reading material in each classroom, students become aware of many of the intangible aspects of reading that are so important:

a. All of their teachers value reading.

b. The content area discipline is one that extends beyond the limits of the core curriculum and textbook into the world of printed materials that people read every day for many purposes.

c. There is an interdisciplinary quality to the traditionally defined subjects in the school curriculum. Literary treatments of scientific and social studies content, scientific approaches to social issues, and examinations of the social and cultural effects of technological advances (among the many possibilities for interdisciplinary viewpoints) can broaden students' perspectives.

d. Students' personal interests, both within and across content areas, are important to their teachers.

Fifth, wide reading has long been valued as one way of enhancing students' skills in reading. Researchers with psycholinguistic and information-processing perspectives on the reading process contend that, all other things being equal, readers with the most experience and background in a subject bring more to the printed page, interact with it more meaningfully, come away from their reading with better understanding and retention, and exhibit greater critical and appreciative insight (9, 22, 45). Similarly, the possibility that wide reading helps students gain in knowledge of and perspective on a subject, even though the gain may not be important or relevant to a particular course, is an important factor. While empirical studies suggest that the measurable effects of wide reading on the variables of vocabulary acquisition and comprehension achievement (as measured by typical norm-referenced tests) are neglible (37, 38) or at best hard to determine when contrasted with direct skill instruction, there are as yet many untested potential benefits to wide reading. For instance, the effects of wide reading on performance in and attitude toward particular content subjects need to be explored further.

Sixth, use of a starter shelf can contribute to the development of the whole child—a well rounded person. The exposure to general knowledge and extensive vocabulary acquired through incidental means like wide reading in topics of interest can strengthen students' strategies for coping with the adult world.

Seventh, the encouragement of wide reading in the junior and senior high years is of critical importance; results from many studies have consistently shown that voluntary reading tends to drop off significantly during these years (28). However, a few carefully designed and conducted studies indicate that this pattern is not inevitable. LaBrant and Heller (32), for instance, demonstrated the value and effectiveness of maximizing conditions for extensive, voluntary reading and, in a follow-up study, LaBrant (33) found that students participating in the original study were reading significantly more twenty years later than similar subjects who did not participate. If we are to have a reading adult public, we must continue to nurture the wide reading habit in secondary schools as is done in many elementary classrooms.

Selecting Material for the Starter Shelf

The choice of the term *starter shelf* is a deliberate one for three reasons. First, the books selected are meant to get students started on voluntary reading habits. Second, the teacher makes the initial selections, with students contributing to the process at a later time. Finally, the initial selections do not become a static, self-contained collection of books. The amount and kind of books will vary from year to year, and from topic to topic in any given year. Teachers should adhere to certain general criteria in making initial selections:

a. Selecting in areas of interest to secondary students.
b. Selecting topics appropriate to the content area.
c. Selecting books of appropriate difficulty level.
d. In most cases, selecting paperbacks or inexpensive hardbacks. (Art collections might be one notable exception to this criterion.)
e. Selecting a small number of books, generally 50-100.

However, beyond these criteria, many possibilities may be considered. For instance, many teachers may want to start out with a broad sampling of titles, choosing relatively few books per topic, but covering the major topics in a given course of study. Other selection patterns that have been successful include:

a. Selecting only those books that would be relevant to the themes and topics taught in the first ten weeks of the school year.
b. Selecting books to provide extended reading in areas treated lightly in class content.
c. Selecting books that examine current and/or controversial issues, for example Native American land claims, the Equal Rights Amendment, sociobiology, animal communication, changes in the English language, or the role of computers in our lives.
d. Selecting books on topics of specific regional interest.

Once a decision has been made on the types of books needed, teachers should turn to some of the many resources currently available for selection books. As the starter shelf will initially consist of relatively few books, it is wise to limit the initial selection process to relatively few teacher resources. The sources listed below have been most useful to the greatest number of teachers in the greatest number of situations over the years. (These as well as additional sources are described in this paper under the heading "Keeping Abreast of New Books.")

    1. The school librarian. Librarians can be a great help in establishing a starter shelf, especially if teachers can specify what they want. It would be useful to make an appointment to explain the process of establishing a starter shelf. The librarian may then share paperback catalogs, locate annotated bibliographies of books, and suggest appropriate books that are already in the library holdings.

    2. NCTE bibliographies. The National Council of Teachers of English has published three annotated bibliographies that are extremely useful and up to date. *Adventuring with Books*, K-8 (1977); *Your Reading* (1975), junior high orientation; and *Books for You* (1976), senior high orientation, all contain annotations of high interest books on topics of relevance to all curricular areas.

    3. *Good Reading for Poor Readers* (1974). Spache's frequent revisions of this book include not only trade books on many topics, but also descriptions of instructional materials, magazines and newspapers, book clubs, series books, and other bibliographies. In addition, there are useful chapters on bibliotherapy, readability assessment, and factors to consider in choosing books.

    4. *Books and the Teenage Reader* (1971). In this revised edition, Carlsen describes in some depth the major types of reading material that interest adolescents, arranged in a developmental sequence, with many examples of each type listed.

If in some cases enough relevant books cannot be found in these sources, the other sources listed in this paper should be consulted. Once a core list has been selected, the books should be ordered. It is also useful at this time to begin collecting publishers' catalogs and other bibliographies, and to begin monitoring the many education journals that review new releases for adolescents.

Initiating Use of the Starter Shelf

Once the books have arrived, the process of matching books and readers begins. It is critical in this early stage for students to be assured that they are *not required* to read books from the starter shelf. If they realize that teachers have a "hidden agenda" in supplying extra books for the classroom, many students may never freely pursue an interest for fear of being required to read more books at a later date or being held accountable for the contents of their free reading for course credit. The following procedures are recommended for introducing the shelf.

The first day. Set aside a class period for the introduction. Apprise students of the purposes and content of the starter shelf, emphasizing that the materials are available for their use on a purely voluntary basis, and that all the books relate in some way to the topics and themes of one content area. Next, enlist the aid of the students in setting up the starter shelf. If many topics and genres are represented in the initial collection, students can help to categorize and shelve books for easy reference. It is helpful to place a bookshelf or wire book rack in an easily accessible part of the room. If it is possible to display the books so that more than the spines are visible, this should be done. Otherwise, extra steps should be taken to acquaint students with the books.

The first week. First day contact with the books may stimulate some students to check out books, ask questions about what is available, or suggest other titles or types of books to order. However, it is important to follow up this initial experience with brief "book meetings" throughout the rest of the week. Five to ten minutes can be taken at the end of class to introduce books by reading synopses of the books, connecting book topics to student experiences, and reading "grabber passages" (47) to stimulate interest. Another effective means of introducing books is for teachers to pick up a book to read early in the week and report on it at length at the end of the week. During this first week, a simple record keeping system should be established. An index card might be placed inside each book with room for each student to record name, date, and short evaluative comment. If students feel the need to find out more about a book before reading it, they may solicit further comments from those who have previously read it. Similarly, if students want to respond fully to a book, through writing or other means, they should be given the opportunity, but it shouldn't be required. The purposes of record keeping—to keep track of books and to determine usage patterns—should be the criteria for determining the record keeping method. At the end of the first week, students should be reminded that the starter shelf is only a beginning collection and they can contribute significantly to the development of the collection.

The first month. During the second, third, and fourth weeks of using the starter shelf, teachers should continue "book meetings" at least once a week. In addition, teachers should encourage students who are reading books from the shelf to contribute their comments. By the end of the month, it will also be necessary to take stock of usage patterns. Books should be checked to find out which have received heavy use, and student rosters should be checked to see which students have read very little or not at all. A class poll might be conducted at this stage to find out what titles or topics would be welcome additions. If certain books are in enough demand to warrant ordering extra copies, this should be noted. Students who have shown little or no interest should be approached individually on an informal basis to find out if there are special needs they would like satisfied. In keeping with the spirit of the starter shelf concept, these students should not be forced to choose a book or topic. It is possible that some of these students are reading books related to other content areas if many other teachers in the school have classroom libraries. It is also possible that some students will not want to read anything outside of the required course materials. For these students, forcing them to read "voluntary" material would be not only self-contradictory, but also self-defeating.

After this stocktaking stage, teachers should decide which books to order to add to the starter shelf. It is recommended that extra books that are in heavy use and books for the more reluctant readers receive priority. For the students who are reading willingly, arrange for extra time in the library to locate books, and consult bibliographies cited in this paper (preferably with individual students) to compile lists of books that might be found at the public library or in a bookstore.

Finally, arrange with the school librarian to borrow a selection of books related to the next topic or unit to be introduced in class. As a part of the introduction to the unit, describe the library books available and mention that they will temporarily be considered a part of the starter shelf.

The second month. Basic procedures for introducing books should be continued into the second month. However, teachers should begin to solicit more student comments on books that have been read. While general evaluative comments are always of value, teachers may also want to focus attention on topics to come in the course, asking students who have read books on these topics to offer their ideas, or mentioning the topics to come and asking if anyone has read something recently that is related.

In addition, an interest inventory adapted for use in the content area should be administered. The inventory can include questions related to past use of the starter shelf, desires for new books, and potential choices for books on topics to come in the course. It is not recommended that an interest inventory of a general nature (*31*: 271-273) be used, nor is it recommended that the inventory be given at the beginning of the year, as is commonly done. As a part of the starter shelf concept, a more limited, focused, inventory used at a later date will be more useful. The rationale for an adapted use of the interest inventory is based on three factors. First, there are many other preinstructional diagnostic procedures that should be done at the beginning of the year. Second, many students respond in a superficial manner to group interest inventories, perhaps because they are not sure for what purposes their responses will be used, or because there has been little relationship between past experiences in filling out similar forms and the reading material they have been given. Third, in relation to reading in a given content area, many students will not know at the beginning of the year what they will be interested in reading. Giving students a chance to get accustomed to the purposes of the starter shelf and to the typical content and procedures of the course, and giving them a chance to clarify their thoughts on what they would like to read about for personal purposes, may provide more valuable data for teachers to use in decision making.

Results of the interest inventory and other informal, observational data obtained by teachers should be used to 1) add to the starter shelf permanent collection, 2) supplement the starter shelf with library books, and 3) begin planning for books to loan students over the Thanksgiving and/or Christmas holidays.

Capitalizing on Student Interest in the Starter Shelf

Once students willingly begin to choose reading material from the starter shelf, teachers should initiate some of the procedures and activities listed to capitalize on this interest through greater involvement with books. In keeping with other aspects of this paper, suggestions in this section are noninstructional and require little classroom time.

1. Nontraditional and creative ideas for book reporting have long been favorite subjects of reading and language arts journal articles. Most ideas are intended for use with elementary school pupils. While some of these ideas may be adapted sensibly to fit the needs of secondary content area classes, many seem trivial, childish, or antithetical to the goals of content area instruction. However, one source (5) lists "61 Ways to Tell about Books," most of which seem appropriate for students in grades seven through twelve.

2. Memberships in student book clubs offered by many publishers provide monthly descriptions of paperbacks that students may buy at discount rates. Book clubs offered by Scholastic, Xerox, and Weekly Reader are particularly good.

3. Raising money to buy paperbacks can be coupled with the Reading is Fundamental (RIF) program which matches 75 percent of any nonfederal money raised for inexpensive books that become the property of students. A complete information packet describing participation in this program is available from RIF headquarters. The Combined Paperback Book Exhibit in Schools may be contacted for information on setting up book fairs on school grounds. The Bureau of Independent Publishers and Distributors (BIPAD) operates through local distributors to supply many paperbacks at discount prices. Gillespie and Spirt (20) list 261 distributors in 46 states that participate in BIPAD. Fink and Bogart (15) and Bogart (4) describe programs of total school involvement in the purchase, reading, and discussion of paperbacks in selected New Jersey schools. Eble and Renton (12) describe the objectives and procedures of a wide reading program in an Ohio secondary school. Paperbacks worth $3500 were purchased and distributed under a federally funded project. Sources of funds are listed at the end of the article.

4. Engage interested students in the process of monitoring new books appearing on the market. Students may be

asked to follow a specific interest, or to catalog books of general interest to all students in the content area course.

5. Investigate the possibilities for using different media to introduce, support, or extend voluntary reading. The journal, *Media and Methods*, is a valuable source regularly featuring such suggestions. Caedmon has many high quality recordings, especially in the area of literature.

Of course, TV/movie tie-ins with books have been used successfully and often. McKenzie (*35*) verified the intuitions of many teachers when she found that 35 of the 50 books most popular with adolescents in her survey were tied to TV or movie productions. Gallo (*16*) found that 62 percent of the students he surveyed were motivated to read a book from having seen movie adaptations. Hamilton (*26*) suggests TV-related books and ways to use them that capitalize on this interest. Although tie-ins may seem to be a more natural approach for English than other content areas because of the large number of current and classic novels adapted for film, there are many possibilities for other content areas. Regularly occurring programs such as Jacques Cousteau, Nova, and the National Geographic specials provide possibilities for science classes. Social studies classes may capitalize on not only current events but also the many historical shows on TV. Even shows with marginal quality may provide springboards to reading. For instance, "In Search of . . . ," a half hour show on unexplained phenomema, is often sketchy in substance but is intriguing. Students may find stimulation in more in-depth, book length treatments of such topics as the monoliths of the British Isles or the question of the existence of the Sasquatch. Valuable, if informal, lessons in critical reading, comparisons of TV versus book treatments of a subject, and consideration of the limits of two contrasting media may help. A selective scanning of *TV Guide* or similar publication can alert teachers and students to upcoming shows of interest, so that books might be available at the appropriate time.

6. Students may prepare a presentation for younger readers. The presentation may be thematic or topical, focusing on a selling job for a number of books in the students' interest areas but of an appropriate difficulty level for younger readers. In a different vein, the presentation may be a prepared reading of one book.

7. Some students may enjoy preparing tapes of favorite passages, exciting parts, that would capture peer interest, or personal comments on what they thought of a book or books.

8. Teachers may wish to guide students in an examination of their characteristic patterns of selection, in an attempt to broaden or deepen interests or to guide students toward more substantial reading.

9. In certain special cases, attempts to guide students in the bibliotherapeutic process may be successful. *The Bookfinder* (1977) and *Reading Ladders for Human Relations* (1972) are especially useful resources. Ideally, students move through stages of identification, catharsis, and insight (Spache, 1974) and finally to action upon their personal circumstances if bibliotherapy is effective. It is unclear, however, whether certain personality types move through these stages better in nondirected versus directed reading settings (5).

10. Many teachers have found that Sustained Silent Reading (SSR) is adaptable in some form to secondary content areas (*34*). As secondary students can generally sustain their reading for longer periods of time than elementary students, a satisfying adaptation of this procedure may require a considerable portion of class time. Nevertheless, SSR has been useful as a way of capitalizing on student interest in voluntary reading as well as in generating that interest.

11. Students may want to start collecting newspaper and magazine articles for special topic files for the classroom, or may wish to collect similar material for themselves. (If teachers are interested in incorporating appropriate magazines and newspapers with the starter shelf paperbacks, they should see Spache's *Good Reading for Poor Readers* for an extensive listing.)

12. Keeping journal records of reading reactions may be an appropriate activity for some students. If journals are used in this manner, teachers should encourage students to share their writing. Teachers' responses should focus on ideas expressed, recommendations for further reading, and similar matters.

13. Ask students to do a selling job in another class on the purposes, procedures, and advantages of the starter shelf. (While total school coordination of the process of establishing and using starter shelves is desirable, many teachers may not

want to participate. A success story or two may help convince both teachers and students of the advantages that can be gained.)

Keeping Abreast of New Books

It cannot be overemphasized that students' past choices and their comments on books, authors, and themes of current interest provide valuable information to teachers for expanding the starter shelf. Furthermore, many of the activities suggested in the previous section of this paper may reveal more books of interest. However, many published sources are also useful. Bibliographic information is provided below under four categories:

1. Sources for Initial Selection
2. Further Sources of General Interest
3. Sources of Interest to Specific Content Areas
4. Older Sources of General Interest

It is strongly recommended that teachers concentrate on Section 1 to establish a beginning collection as described in this paper. During the process of initial selection, the sources in Sections 2 and 3 should be collected or located. Future selections generally should come from these sources. Finally, the sources in Section 4 should be consulted. Although these sources were published before 1970, many high quality books not listed in the newer bibliographies may be found in the sources in Section 4.

Section 1   Sources for Initial Selection

- The school librarian.
- NCTE Bibliographies. (Copublished by Citation Press and Scholastic Magazines.)
- Ciancolo, Patricia. *Adventuring with Books: A Booklist for Pre-K-Grade 8. Urbana, Illinois: NCTE, 1977.*
- Donelson, Kenneth L. *Books for You: A Booklist for Senior High Students*. Urbana, Illinois: 1976.
- Walker, Jerry. *Your Reading: A Booklist for Junior High Students. Urbana, Illinois: 1975.*
- Spache, George. *Good Reading for Poor Readers*, Ninth Edition. Champaign, Illinois: Garrard, 1974.

• Carlesen, G. Robert. *Books and the Teenage Reader*, Revised Edition, New York: Bantam Books, 1971.

Section 2.   Further Sources of General Interest

All of the following sources have been published since 1970 and list or describe books appropriate for many content areas.

American Library Association. *Best Books for Young Adults*. Young Adult Services Division, 50 East Huron Street, Chicago 60611. Annual listing based on votes of librarians in the United States.

American Library Association. *High Interest Low Reading Level Information Packet*. Young Adult Services Division. Articles and bibliographies on identifying and evaluating appropriate high/low books for adolescents.

American Library Association. *Still Alive: Best of the Best, 1960-1974*. Young Adult Services Division, ALA, Chicago, 1975. Reevaluations of the ALA "Best Books" annual reports 1960-1974 in view of their appropriateness for adolescent readers in 1975.

ALAN. *Assembly on Literature for Adolescents*—NCTE. A special interest group of the NCTE, ALAN Newsletter regularly reviews new books appropriate for adolescents, and features comments on new developments in the field of literature for adolescents, and features comments on new developments in the field of literature for adolescents. Editorial Offices, 125 Aderhold Hall, College of Education, University of Georgia, Athens, Georgia 30602.

Baskins, Barbara. *Notes from a Different Drummer*. New York: Bowker, 1977. Over 400 books focusing on the disabled or those with special needs are categorized and annotated. Books are coded as being appropriate for the young child, mature child, young adolescent, or mature adolescent.

Bernstein, Joanne. *Books to Help Children Cope with Separation and Loss*. New York: Bowker, 1977. 438 titles are categorized and annotated.

Books for the Teen Age. New York Public Library, Office of Young Adult Services, 8 East 40 Street, New York 10016. Annual listing, annotated.

Booklist. A semimonthly journal featuring about 150 book reviews per issue. American Library Association, 50 E. Huron Street, Chicago 60611.

Book Review Digest. Monthly, with annual cumulative issues. H. W. Wilson Company, 950 University Avenue, Bronx, New York 10452.

Bulletin of the Center for Children's Books. A monthly review of both children's and adolescent's books. University of Chicago Press, 5801 Ellis Avenue, Chicago 60637.

Burton, Dwight. *Literature Study in the High Schools,* third edition. New York: Holt, Rinehart and Winston, 1970, 327-341. A short bibliography and discussion of biography, personalized views of historical events, and true adventures appropriate for adolescents.

Dreyer, Sharon. *The Bookfinder.* Circle Pines, Minnesota: American Guidance Service, 1977. An excellent resource in terms of organization, comprehensiveness, and ease of use. Annotates books for children aged two through fifteen by subject area, with special emphasis on problems of coping and growing to maturity. (Useful for counseling/bibliotherapeutic approaches to using books.)

Fader, Daniel. *Hooked on Books.* New York: Berkeley Publishing, 1976. See "The Reading List: A Thousand Authors."

Golden Books for Students with Reading Problems. New York: Western Publishing, 1976. Annotated list, coded for reading difficulty from primary to secondary levels.

The Horn Book. Horn Book, Park Square Building, 31 St. James Avenue, Boston, 02116. A semimonthly. See the columns on new books for each season and "Outlook Tower," a column on current adult books of interest to high school readers and, occasionally, books published for teenagers.

Index to Young Readers' Collective Biographies. New York: Bowker, 1971. Biographical books and other material on over 4,000 famous people.

International Reading Association Journals. *The Reading Teacher,* elementary orientation and *Journal of Reading,* secondary orientation, frequently feature articles and reviews of appropriate books for adolescents.

Journal of Education, February 1978. School of Education, Boston University. Catalogs over 600 high interest books for school-age readers.

Junior High School Library Catalog. New York: H.W. Wilson, 1970. Brief reviews of over 3,400 books.

Klein, Celeste, and Doris Hiatt. *Kliatt Paperback Book Guide,* 6 Crocker Circle, West Newton, Massachusetts 02165. A quarterly publication reviewing approximately 1,000 books per year under five headings: The Arts, Literature, Social Studies, Reference, and Miscellaneous.

Library Journal and *School Library Journal*. R.R. Bowker, 1180 Avenue of the Americas, New York 10036. Both published semimonthly.

National Council of Teachers of English Journals. *Language Arts* (formerly *Elementary English*), elementary orientation and *English Journal*, secondary orientation, both include regular columns on new books.

New York Times Sunday Book Review has devoted more space in recent years to books for children and adolescents. May be purchased separately at many bookstores.

Reid, Virginia. *Reading Ladders for Human Relations*, fifth edition. Washington, D.C.: American Council on Education, 1972. Extensive listing of books, annotated and categorized according to the kinds of problems school-aged children confront. Useful for counseling (bibliotherapeutic approaches to using books).

Russell, Norma. "Popular Nonfiction Titles for Adolescents," *Arizona English Bulletin*, 18, 3 (April 1976) 48-59.

Senior High School Library Catalog, tenth edition. New York: H.W. Wilson, 1972. Brief reviews of over 4,750 titles.

SIGNAL Special Interest Group, A Network on Adolescent Literature, a newsletter affiliated with the IRA, includes summaries of many books and occasional comments on using literature for the adolescent. 530 Lac La Belle Drive, Oconomowoc, Wisconsin 53066.

Top of the News, quarterly journal of the ALA with emphases on books for children and adolescents.

University of Iowa, Annual Books for Young Adults Poll. BYA poll, Books for Young Adults, W. 312 East Hall, University of Iowa, Iowa City, Iowa 52242. Favorite choices of Iowa high school readers.

White, Marian. *High Interest-Easy Reading for Junior and Senior High School Students*. Urbana, Illinois: NCTE, 1972. (Copublished by Citation Press and Scholastic Magazines.)

Withrow, Dorothy (Ed.), *Gateways to Readable Books*, fifth edition. Bronx, New York: H.W. Wilson, 1975. Over 1,000 titles for reluctant and poor reading adolescents are categorized and annotated.

Note. The current catalogs of major paperback publishers are valuable resources to add to a growing file of books for the starter shelf. In addition, many paperback publishers (for instance Bantam, Dell, Doubleday, Scholastic) provide study guides for some of their titles and other supplementary material. A Gillespie and Spirt publication (20) contains extensive comments on services available from the major paperback publishers.

Section III: Sources of Interest to Specific Content Areas

ART

- Hafner, Lawrence. *Developmental Reading in Middle and Secondary Schools*. New York: Macmillan, 1977, 460-463.
- Marantz, Kenneth (Ed.). *A Bibliography of Children's Art Literature*. Washington, D.C.: National Education Association, 1965.
- Roe, Betty, Barbara Stoodt, and Paul Burns. *Reading Instruction in the Secondary School*. Chicago: Rand McNally, 1978, 317-318.
- Smith, Ron. *Guide to Post Classical Works of Art, Literature, and Music Based on Myths of the Greeks and Romans*. Urbana, Illinois: NCTE, 1976.
- Thomas, Ellen L., and H. Alan Robinson. *Improving Reading in Every Class*, second edition. Boston: Allyn and Bacon, 1977, 395-401. Chapter 16, "Fine Arts," while not suggesting specific titles, provides valuable directions in the unique problems of establishing an art room book collection.

MATHEMATICS

- Earle, Richard. *Teaching Reading and Mathematics*. Newark, Delaware: International Reading Association, 1976. Appendix on "High Interest Materials for Mathematics Classrooms," 79-84.
- Hardgrove, Clarence. *The Elementary and Junior High School Mathematics Library*. Washington, D.C.: National Council of Teachers of Mathematics, 1975 (see also 1973 edition).
- NCTM. *The High School Mathematics Library*, third edition. Washington, D.C.: National Council of Teachers of Mathematics, 1967.
- Roe, Stoodt, and Burns, 1978, 269-270.

- Thomas, Della. *And More to Grow ... Mathematics and the School Library*, revised edition. Library Education Department, Oklahoma State University Library, 1963.

PHYSICAL EDUCATION/SPORTS

- Bentz, Donald. "Sports Books, Grade Seven Up," *Junior Libraries*, 6 (November 1959), 11-13.
- Hafner, 1977, 477.
- Mitchell, Viola, Julia Robberson, and June Obley. *Camp Counseling*, fifth edition. Philadelphia: W.B. Saunders, 1977. Chapter bibliographies contain extensive lists of books on all aspects of camping including first aid, cooking, equipment, and survival.
- Patlak, Sanford. "Sandy's 99 Sports Books for Reluctant Readers," in H.A. Robinson and E.L. Thomas (Eds.), *Fusing Reading Skills and Content*. Newark, Delaware: International Reading Association, 1969, 201-204.
- Roe, Stoodt, Burns, 1978, 307.
- Russell, Noma, "Popular Nonfiction Titles for Adolescents," *Arizona English Bulletin*, 18 (April 1976), 53-54, sports choices.

SCIENCE

- AAAS *Science Booklist for Young Adults*. American Association for the Advancement of Science, 1515 Massachusetts Avenue, Washington, D.C. 20005, 1970.
- AAAS *Science Booklist Supplement*. Update of 1970 edition. Annotated listings by category, including mathematics titles. Emphasis on junior and senior high readers (1978).
- AAAS *Science Books and Films*. A quarterly journal reviewing books for elementary, high school, and adult readers.
- Gott, Margaret, and James Wailes (Compilers). "High Interest-Low Vocabulary Science Books," reading level 1-4 for older readers. Boulder, Colorado: Bureau of Educational Research, University of Colorado, 1970.
- "Views on Science Books," *The Horn Book*. A regular column in each issue, with annotations and keyed interest levels, elementary through high school.

SOCIAL STUDIES

- The Asia Society. *Asia: A Guide to Paperbacks*, 112 E. 64 Street, New York 10021, 1968. Fiction and nonfiction written for students in high school, annotated and categorized by geographical region.

- Carpenter, Helen. *Gateways to American History: An Annotated Grade List of Books For Slow Learners*. New York: H.W. Wilson, 1968. Arranged by historical period.
- Fleener, Charles, and Ron Seckinger. *The Guide to Latin American Paperback Literature*. Gainesville, Florida: Center for Latin American Studies, 1966. Describes over 650 fiction and nonfiction books and pamphlets.
- Hershowitz, Herbert, and Bernard Marlin. *A Guide to Reading in American History: The Unit Approach*. New York, Signet, 1966. Over 1,000 adult nonfiction paperbacks annotated with levels of difficulty from average secondary to graduate level.
- Inkster, Norma. "An Annotated Bibliography of Recent Fiction about National Americans for Young People in Grades 7 through 12," *Arizona English Bulletin*, 18 (April 1976), 194-198.
- *Interracial Books for Children*. Published quarterly, reviews books primarily appropriate for nonwhite children. Council on Interracial Books for Children, 9 E. 40 Street, New York 10016.
- Metzner, Seymour. *World History in Juvenile Books: A Geographical and Chronological Guide*. New York: H.W. Wilson, 1973. Contains 2,700 fiction and nonfiction titles for average and below average secondary students. Also by Metzner, *American History in Juvenile Books: A Chronological Guide*, 1965. Over 2,000 titles.
- NCSS. *World Civilization Booklist: Supplementary Reading for Secondary Schools*.
  American History Booklist for High Schools: A Selection for Supplementary Reading.
  World History Booklist.
  Children's Books to Enrich the Social Studies (Helen Huus). Washington, D.C.: National Council for the Social Studies.
  NCTE. Stensland, Anna Lee. *Literature by and about the American Indian: An Annotated Bibliography*, 1973. (Revised Spring 1979.)
- Ortego, Philip. *Mexican American Literature*, 1976.
- Rollins, Charlemae. *We Build Together: A Reader's Guide to Negro Life and Literature for Elementary and High School Use*, 1967.
- Spache, George, *Good Reading for the Disadvantaged Reader: Multiethnic Resources*. Champaign Illinois: Garrard, 1970.

- Tooze, Ruth, and Beatrice Krone. *Literature and Music as Resources for Social Studies*. Englewood Cliffs, New Jersey: Prentice-Hall, 1965.
- United States Committee for UNICEF.
  Africa, 1968.
  Latin America, 1969.
  Near East and North Africa, 1970.
  Annotated bibliographies on a wide range of materials.

VOCATIONAL
- ALA. *Vocations in Biography and Fiction*. Chicago: American Library Association, 1967. Appropriate for senior high.
- Kuder, G.F., and L.E. Crawford. *Kuder Book List*. Chicago: Science Research Associates, 1959. Books with a reading difficulty range of fifth to eleventh grade are categorized by interest areas measured on Kuder Interest Inventory.
- Roe, Stoodt, and Burns, 297.
- Schuman, Patricia. *Materials for Occupational Education: An Annotated Source Guide*. New York: Bowker, 1971.
- Thomas and Robinson, 339-341.

OTHER
- Hafner, 1977. Music, 472-473.
- Roe, Stoodt, and Burns. Home Economics, 304-305; Driver Education, 315-316; Music, 320.

Section IV   *Older Sources of General Interest*
- ALA. "Easy Adult Books for Slow High School Readers," *Top of the News*, 17 (December 1960), 19-21.
- California State Committee on Development Reading. "Graded Reading List," *Bulletin of the National Association of Secondary School Principals*, 34 (February 1950), 111-124. Nonfiction books for poor readers, grades 7-9.
- Dunn, Anita, Mabel Jachman, and Roy Newton. *Fare for the Reluctant Reader*, third edition. Albany: State University of New York. Books for students, grades 7-12.
- Emery, Raymond, and Margaret Houshower. *High Interest—Easy Reading for Junior and Senior High Reluctant Readers*. Champaign, Illinois: NCTE, 1965.
- Hunt, Jacob. "Easy Nonfictional Materials for the Handicapped Reader," *High School Journal*, 39 (March 1956), 322-323. Books on many topics appropriate for secondary school students.

- Hunt, Jacob. "Easy and Interesting Fiction for the Handicapped Reader," *High School Journal*, 39 (April 1956), 378-385.
- Kress, Roy. *A Place to Start*. Syracuse, New York: The Reading Center, Syracuse University, 1963. Books for retarded readers, elementary through high school.
- Sprague, Lois. "Nonfiction Books for Retarded Readers in the Upper Grades," *Elementary English*, 28 (January 1951), 28-34.
- Strang, Ruth, E. Phelps, and D. Withrow. *Gateways to Readable Books: An Annotated Graded List of Books in Many Fields for Adolescents with Reading Difficulty*, fourth edition. H.W. Wilson Company, 1966.
- Whitenach, Carolyn, and Alex Caughran. "For the Reluctant Reader," *NEA Journal*, 47 (December 1958), 644, 652.

Integrating Paperbacks with Regular Instruction

It is important to reiterate that the major purpose of the starter shelf is to stimulate greater voluntary reading among adolescents in content-related material. This is a valid objective of secondary reading in and of itself. If students encounter too many requirements for "voluntary" reading, they may never develop the intrinsic motivation to read on their own. If, however, a willing wide reading habit develops among students, it can be capitalized upon in many ways in the course of classroom instruction. The suggestions that follow are not intended to be comprehensive—that would be beyond the scope of this paper—but are meant to suggest uses for paperbacks.

1. *Booktalks*. Burkhardt et al. (7) describe the procedures they use to conduct teacher-guided discussions of paperbacks that eighth grade students choose to read. Once a month, students choose one book to read from a selected list provided by the school. At the end of the month, students who have selected the same book participate in a discussion under teacher leadership. All eighth grade teachers and administrative staff are involved in leading the booktalks. As two periods are set aside on booktalk days, students may attend either two discussion groups if two books were read, or one discussion group and a multimedia presentation designed to stimulate interest in other books available to students. Teachers attempt

to integrate vocabulary and comprehension instruction with the booktalk.

For further ideas on preparing for and conducting both group and individual booktalks, the following sources may be of value: Edwards (*13*), Gillespie (*17*), Gillespie and Lembo (*18, 19*), Walker (*48, 49, 50*).

2. *Building a unit around a common paperback.* Often, topics of importance in the curriculum may be approached by an initial reading and discussion of a paperback, with the core text serving as a supplementary resource for selective reading. For instance, *Across Five Aprils* (or any of a number of other fictional, historical, or personal accounts) could be used to introduce a Civil War unit. Students then might read the text selectively to develop a timeline for events in the Civil War, and individual or small group culminating activities could be provided to add more substance to the unit content.

3. *Following up a unit with small group reading of many paperbacks.* At the conclusion of a unit, teachers can lead their students in generating a list of topics they would like to explore further. Small groups of three to five could be formed to read a common book for reporting to the whole class, or to read many sources on their topic. In this approach it is especially useful to have books on a wide variety of readability levels in order to provide all students with material they can understand.

4. *Building a unit that encompasses multiple texts.* There are many ways to design multiple text units. For example, teachers have frequently selected books of different difficulty levels on the same topic, books with different perspectives on the same issue or theme, or books that provide in-depth treatment of subtopics. Donlan (*10*) has described the use of "participation guides" to help manage multitext units, and Handlin (*27*) gives an anecdotal account of group discussions based on students' individual readings of different books. Many other useful ideas may be found in *Arizona English Bulletin*, April 1976; Spann and Culp (*46*); and *English Journal*, February 1979.

5. *Guided individualized reading.* Many adaptations of the individualized reading principles of self-selection, self-pacing, and conferencing have been tried in the secondary schools. One particularly useful approach (*3*) included the use

of guides on 43 discussion topics, duplicated for student use in planning conferences with the teacher.

6. *Student initiated units.* Teachers may organize units that capitalize on student interest in the starter shelf by analyzing patterns of student choice and designing a unit that will facilitate careful investigation of topics the students have indicated are important through their reading choices. The possibilities for active student involvement in a unit designed in this way are greater than for units integrating material for which students have not expressed interest. Another way of approaching student-initiated units, described elsewhere in greater detail (2), is to involve students in deciding on unit topics, content, and procedures.

These six suggestions are only examples of the types of patterns in which the reading of many paperbacks can be incorporated into curricular goals. Many other possibilities are suggested in Gillespie and Spirt (21). Beneficial side effects of implementing starter shelves are that teachers may discover new books to use in their content classrooms and unique approaches to the use of multiple texts in their courses.

Summary

A procedure has been presented for stimulating greater voluntary reading of high interest books relevant to the content areas. Emphasis has been placed on noninstructional use of the starter shelf in order to accentuate the importance of developing willing, lifetime readers. The rationale for the starter shelf has been provided and a number of suggestions for selecting books, initiating their use, and following up on their use have been provided. It is assumed that many teachers will find interesting variations on this procedure when it is initiated, and will be able to tailor a program to fit the unique needs of their students. The thoughts of an educator written over eighty years ago seem appropriate:

> The danger to be dreaded is that reading grow perfunctory, a task done to please the teacher, not spontaneous, not impelled by inner motive.— Samuel Thurber, "How To Make the Study of Literature Interesting," *The School Review*, September 1898.

References

1. BARRILLEAUX, LOUIS. "Textbook and Library Usage in Junior High Science," in Duggins (Comp.), *Teaching Reading for Human Values in High School.* Columbus, Ohio: Merrill, 1972, 304-311.
2. BISHOP, DAVID. "Involving Students in Unit Planning in Subject Area Classes," *Ohio Reading Teacher,* 13, 3 (Spring 1978), 20-25.
3. BLOW, BARBARA. "Individualized Reading," *Arizona English Bulletin,* 18, 3 (April 1976), 151-153.
4. BOGART, M. "Paperback Books in New Jersey," in Vivienne Anderson (Ed.), *Paperbacks in Education.* New York: Teachers College Press, Columbia University, 1966.
5. BROWN, ELEANOR. *Bibliotherapy and Its Widening Applications.* Metuchen, New Jersey: Scarecrow Press, 1975.
6. BUREAU OF INDEPENDENT PUBLISHERS AND DISTRIBUTORS, 122 E. 42 Street, New York 10017.
7. BURKHARDT, D., et al. "Marilyn Monroe and Even More—An Unusual Approach to Reading," presentation at the Annual Convention of the College Reading Association, 1977.
8. COMBINED PAPERBACK BOOK EXHIBIT, Scarborough Park, Albany Post Road, Briarcliff Manor, New York 10510.
9. COOPER, CHARLES, and ANTHONY PETROSKY. "A Psycholinguistic View of the Fluent Reading Process," *Journal of Reading,* 20, 3 (December 1976), 184-207.
10. DONLAN, DAN. "Multiple Text Programs in Literature," *Journal of Reading,* 19, 4 (January 1976), 312-319.
11. DUGGINS, JAMES (Comp.). *Teaching Reading for Human Values in High School.* Columbus: Charles E. Merrill, 1972.
12. EBLE, MARY, and JEANNE RENTON. "Books Unlimited: A Schoolwide Reading Program," *Journal of Reading,* 22, 2 (November 1978), 123-130.
13. EDWARDS, MARGARET. *The Fair Garden and the Swarm of Beasts.* New York: Hawthorne, 1969.
14. ESTES, THOMAS, and JOSEPH VAUGHAN. *Reading and Learning in the Content Classroom.* Boston: Allyn and Bacon, 1978.
15. FINK, R., and M. BOGART. *Paperbound Books in New Jersey Public Schools.* Trenton, New Jersey: State Department of Education, 1965.
16. GALLO, DON. "Free Reading and Book Reports—An Informal Survey of Grade Eleven," *Journal of Reading,* 11 (1968), 532-538.
17. GILLESPIE, JOHN. *More Juniorplots.* New York: R.R. Bowker, 1977.
18. GILLESPIE, JOHN, and DIANE LEMBO. *Juniorplots.* New York: R.R. Bowker, 1967.
19. GILLESPIE, JOHN, and DIANE LEMBO. *Introducing Books: A Guide for the Middle Grades.* New York: R.R. Bowker, 1970.
20. GILLESPIE, JOHN, and DIANA SPIRT. *Paperback Books for Young People: An Annotated Guide to Publishers and Distributors.* Chicago: American Library Association, 1972.
21. GILLESPIE, JOHN, and DIANA SPIRT. *The Young Phenomenon: Paperbacks in Our Schools.* Chicago: ALA, 1972.
22. GOODMAN, KENNETH. "Reading: A Psycholinguistic Guessing Game," *Journal of the Reading Specialist,* 6 (May 1967), 126-135.
23. GRAY, WILLIAM S. *The Reading Interests and Habits of Adults.* Chicago: University of Chicago Press, 1935.
24. GRAY, WILLIAM S. *What Makes a Book Readable.* New York: Macmillan, 1929.

25. HAYNES, LAWRENCE. *Developmental Reading in Middle and Secondary Schools*. New York: Macmillan, 1977.
26. HAMILTON, HARLAN. "TV Tie-Ins: Books for an Unhooked Generation," *Arizona English Bulletin*, 18, 3 (April 1976), 107-109.
27. HANDLIN, BERTHA. "Group Discussion of Individualized Reading," *English Journal*, February 1943, 67-74.
28. HARRIS, ALBERT. *How to Increase Reading Ability*, 6th edition. New York: McKay, 1975.
29. HERBER, HAROLD. *Teaching Reading in Content Areas*. Englewood Cliffs, New Jersey: Prentice-Hall, 1970.
30. HERBER, HAROLD. *Teaching Reading in Content Areas*, second edition. Englewood Cliffs, New Jersey: 1978.
31. KARLIN, ROBERT. *Teaching Reading in High School*, third edition. Indianapolis: Bobbs-Merrill, 1977.
32. LABRANT, LOU, and FRIEDA HELLER. *Evaluation of Free Reading in Grades 7 to 12 Inclusive*, Ohio State University Contributions to Education #4. Columbus: OSU Press, 1939.
33. LABRANT, LOU. *The Guinea Pigs after 20 Years*. Columbus: OSU Press, 1961, 127-163.
34. MCCRACKEN, ROBERT. "Do We Want Real Readers?" *Journal of Reading*, 12 (1969), 446-448.
35. MCKENZIE, JOANNA. "A Survey of Leisure Time Reading of Adolescents," *Arizona English Bulletin*, 18, 3 (April 1976), 13-22.
36. PETERS, CHARLES. "How To Get More Comprehensive Reading Programs at the Secondary Level," *Journal of Reading*, 20, 6 (March 1977), 513-519.
37. PETTY, WALTER, C. HEROLD, and E. STOLL. *The State of Knowledge about the Teaching of Vocabulary*, Cooperative Research Project #3128. Champaign, Illinois: NCTE, 1968.
38. PRESTON, RALPH, J. SCHNEYER, and F. THYNG. *Guiding the Social Studies Reading of High School Students*. Washington, D.C.: NCSS, 1963.
39. READING IS FUNDAMENTAL. L'Enfant 2500, Smithsonian Institution, Washington, D.C. 20560.
40. ROBINSON, H. ALAN, and ELLEN L. THOMAS. *Fusing Reading Skills and Content*. Newark, Delaware: International Reading Association, 1969.
41. ROE, BETTY, BARBARA STOODT, and PAUL BURNS. *Reading Instruction in the Secondary Schools*. Chicago: Rand McNally, 1978.
42. SCHULTE, EMERITA. "Independent Reading Interests of Children in Grades 4, 5, and 6," in A.J. Figurel (Ed.), *Reading and Realism*. Newark, Delaware: International Reading Association, 1969, 728-732.
43. SHIRLEY, FEHL. "The Influence of Reading on Concepts, Attitudes, and Behavior," in Duggins (Comp.), *Teaching Reading for Human Values in High School*. Columbus: Merrill, 1972, 46-56.
44. SMITH, CARL, SHARON SMITH, and LARRY MIKULECKY. *Teaching Reading in Secondary School Content Subjects*. New York: Holt, Rinehart and Winston, 1978.
45. SMITH, FRANK. *Understanding Reading*. New York: Holt, Rinehart and Winston, 1971.
46. SPANN, SYLVIA, and MARY BETH CULP. *Thematic Units in Teaching English and the Humanities*. Urbana, Illinois: NCTE, 1975.
47. THOMAS, ELLEN, and H. ALAN ROBINSON. *Improving Reading in Every Class*, second edition. Boston: Allyn and Bacon, 1977.
48. WALKER, ELINOR (Ed.). *Book Bait: Detailed Notes on Adult Books Popular with Young People*. Chicago: ALA, 1957.

49. WALKER, ELINOR (Ed.). *Doors to More Mature Reading: Detailed Notes on Adult Books for Use with Young People.* Chicago: ALA, 1964.
50. WALKER, ELINOR (Ed.). *Book Bait,* second edition. Chicago: ALA, 1969.
51. WAPLES, DOUGLAS, BERNARD BERELSON, and FRANKLYN BRADSHAW. *What Reading Does to People.* Chicago: University of Chicago Press, 1940.

He then is ready to discover the expressive relationship that exists between reading and writing music and reading and **writing language.**—Gertrude B. Corcoran, *Language Experience for Nursery and Kindergarten Years*, 1976

Using Student Publishers to Promote Book Sharing

Betty R. Grant
Central Bucks School District
Chalfont, Pennsylvania

They say that children do not like to write. *They* say that youngsters have lost their sense of imagination. *They* say that schools do not emphasize the second "R." The infallible "they" obviously have not seen a school where a publishing center is in operation. Students *are* motivated to write when a beautifully made book is the end result of their creative efforts.

The rationale underlying the development of the publishing center concept is that children develop meaningful language skills by writing and publishing their own books. The techniques used in the publishing experience integrate all aspects of the language arts curriculum, as well as the creative arts for illustrating and bookmaking. Furthermore, such a program also includes an unwritten theme: that writing and reading should be exciting and, subsequently, motivate students. An important benefit of such a program, which can be carried out in grades K-12, is the sizable self-concept and confidence boost of participants, particularly with the "published" authors.

Developing a Publishing Center

The intent of this paper is to present ideas which individual teachers and/or an entire district can use to motivate writing, publishing, and reading of student-authored books.

A publishing center can successfully utilize any nook in a school. With a little imagination (such as using colorful signs), available space can be converted into a publishing center. Copious space is not a prerequisite, although it is more desirable to work in a large, appropriately equipped location. Some of the most successful centers this writer has observed have functioned admirably in a hallway with a minimum of supplies.

One way to initiate a publishing center program is to enlist the aid of student volunteers. It is imperative to select for this task a core of students with superior language arts skills as well as with good peer relationships. There are several satisfactory alternatives to the volunteer student type of program. Paid school aides, parent volunteers, an entire class (as a service project for the school), or a school publishing club may act successfully as publishers. It is essential that those working at the center attend training sessions before beginning the publishing process with student authors.

Those chosen to be publishers are trained how to read and review manuscripts. Later, these publishers will work with student authors to review their manuscripts. To provide a systematic way of checking each manuscript, checklists (such as the examples shown in figures one and two) may be used. Publishers should remember that student authors should always make final decisions concerning improvement of their written copy. An adult supervisor should check recopied manuscripts before they are bound.

The next steps involve the actual binding of the manuscripts submitted. There are many methods that can be used for the bookmaking process. The age of the children, length of time allocated for the project, materials available, and working space designated for bookmaking must all be considered when selecting a bookmaking technique. (See bibliography on bookmaking techniques.)

A checklist may assist the publisher's task by providing a step-by-step outline of the binding process. One binding method is to place the manuscript in a drilling frame, drill holes along the edge of the manuscript, and sew the pages with strong thread. Next, end papers, spine tape, and a cover are selected by a student author. Authors may choose from many different and creative cover types. Publishers assist the authors in designing a cover which best suits the book's title. Marbling is a very popular cover design used by students. Spatter painting, styrofoam prints, felt scraps, melted crayons, pipe cleaners, and combinations of these techniques may be found in interesting variations on book covers. This points out an advantage of using students as publishers: they have infinite patience as they labor with the young authors at these creative (and often messy) techniques.

Encouraging Creative Writing

In schools where publishing centers are active, teachers encourage creative writing within their classes. Elementary students submit successful manuscripts that have been the result of stimulating classroom experiences such as cooking, conducting an experiment, or responding to a film or art activity. Secondary students may write creatively or compile an interesting factual manuscript. Manuscripts submitted to a center come from any subject area, not just the language arts field. At every level, successful writing is usually preceded by communication about experiences, ideas, and feelings.

Many teachers find it advantageous to keep a folder containing each student's writing efforts. A student, or student and teacher, may periodically review an entire file to determine which stories might be worthy of editing and submitting for publishing. Using this system, teachers are more likely to provide opportunities for their students to engage in meaningful composing on a regularly scheduled basis and students are more likely to write freely as they recognize a purpose for their efforts.

One way to control the quality of manuscripts submitted to a publishing center is to request that a form be filled out by the author's teacher (see example, figure two). It is vital to have a teacher review each manuscript submitted, for this assures that an author is submitting quality writing worthy of the effort that will follow.

If the students (or adults) working at a publishing center have the time and talent to successfully edit manuscripts, teachers need not be encumbered with correcting all manuscripts submitted; hence, a faculty may encourage more writing.

The enthusiasm of a staff will contribute to the positive atmosphere toward writing in a school. Students are motivated to write by teachers who read student authored books to their classes. The first books published at a center should be read aloud and put on display to be admired by all. An initial promotion of the books displayed motivates other students to apply themselves to the task of completing a worthy manuscript.

As more and more books are published, students will read more student authored materials. At the elementary level, students are eager to read their books to their own class and to other classes and to have the book placed on display. In secondary schools, it is considered prestigious to have one's manuscript displayed or cataloged in the library. Binding a student's research paper gives motivation for an otherwise tedious process and provides easy-to-read information for those students who find it difficult to comprehend reference material. Often the most popular volumes in the library, student authored books are rarely lost or overdue. Some librarians may choose to treat them as reference materials and not permit them to be circulated out of the building.

Building Self-Concepts

An important byproduct of a publishing experience is the effect it has on an author's self-concept. Frequently a teacher will notice that a problem student is one of the first to have a book bound at a center. After the publishing experience, disruptive, restless students often feel the pride of authorship and the warmth of acceptance that their efforts bring. The objective of the publishing center then is to develop the students' language skills by having them write and publish their own books. But of equal importance is the boost in self-esteem provided by the experience.

When student publishers are utilized, they acquire invaluable self-confidence during the year, and both publisher and author gain by learning to cooperate. It is amazing how well cross-age groupings can function. The publishing center concept demonstrates how a school's own students may provide a valuable resource.

Young Authors' Day

Another incentive for writing may be provided by establishing a schoolwide or districtwide Young Authors' Conference Day. Teachers may choose the participants from their own classes, or a committee of teachers may choose the participants from a whole school. Another way is to have students choose participants by voting for the best book(s) from their respective classes. One more method is to select carefully a group of students who represent the entire student body to choose participants under the leadership of a librarian, English teacher, or reading specialist. The word "winner" should be avoided in referring to the chosen entries as all manuscripts are praiseworthy.

For individual schools, a typical Young Authors' Day may include recognition of the young authors with an award of merit. Another event may be a talk given by a local professional author to the budding young writers. Students delight in hearing a real author's problems of editing and publishing. Parents may be invited to a reception given for the student authors, during which time students can tell about their books and read favorite portions. Both students and parents enjoy this exchange. Local newspapers will often provide a photographer and news coverage, all of which serves to enhance school-community relations.

A districtwide Young Authors' Conference Day requires coordination by key people in each participating school. The day's schedule, once established, can retain the same format from year to year. A day might consist of registration, book-sharing, picnic lunch, and workshop sessions. Changing the themes yearly for the workshop sessions can provide variety to each year's program. Some ideas for yearly themes are illustration, storytelling, puppetry, nature, and creative dramatics.

There are many alternate ways of providing students with publishing experiences. No matter which model a school uses, teachers find that publishing provides a natural motivation for writing and reading.

A publishing center will be successful with just two essential elements: 1) a dedicated, well-trained core of publishers and 2) faculty cooperation. For the children and their teachers, the rewards of such a program are fantastic.

PEACE VALLEY PUBLISHING CENTER

(Checklist)

Author _____   Teacher_____

Title _____   Date Started _____

Publisher _____

Special publishing instructions _____

CHECKPOINTS FOR EDITING	CHECKPOINTS FOR BINDING
[ ] Read story with author.	[ ] Is it worthy of binding?
[ ] Is it worthy of publishing?	[ ] Does it have margins?
[ ] Make corrections on rough copy.	[ ] Blank pages beginning and end?
_____ Spelling	[ ] Title Page?
_____ Punctuation	[ ] Dedication page? (optional)
_____ Paragraphs	[ ] Table of contents? (optional)
[ ] Plan illustrations to match story.	[ ] Correct order and right direction?
[ ] Use white sheets and writing guide.	[ ] Drill and sew?
[ ] Plan table of contents (optional).	[ ] Choose end papers?
[ ] Add illustrations (colored pencils).	[ ] Choose cover paper?
[ ] Make sure pages are in the correct order.	[ ] Choose spine tape color?
[ ] Add blank pages at beginning and end.	[ ] Get scrap paper for gluing?
[ ] Have Mrs. Grant recheck.	[ ] Attach end papers.
	[ ] Glue brown wrapping paper reinforcement.
	[ ] Cut cover cardboard.
	[ ] Use masking tape to cover cardboard.
	[ ] Attach spine tape.
	[ ] Cut cover paper.
	[ ] Rubber cement cover onto cardboard.
	[ ] Insert manuscript, rubber cement to cardboard cover.
	[ ] Design cover.
Date completed _____	[ ] Stamp and sign back page.
	[ ] Have Mrs. Grant recheck.

Figure 1. Editing and Binding Checklist

Grant

PEACE VALLEY PUBLISHING CENTER

Author _____ Date _____

Grade _____ Teacher _____

Title of Book _____

   Teacher's approval _____ Date _____

     [   ] Has not been proofread.

     [   ] Has been proofread (rough draft).

     [   ] Has been recopied (white paper).

     [   ] Illustrations need to be added (blank pages included).

     [   ] Illustrations completed (colored pencils).

Figure 2.   Manuscript Review

Bibliography

Books for Children
Purdy, Susan. *Books for You to Make.* J.B. Lippincott, 1973.
Weiss, Harvey. *How to Make Your Own Books.* Thomas Y. Crowell, 1974.

Books for Teachers
Darley, Lionel S. *Introduction to Bookbinding.* Faber and Faber, 1965.
Johnson, Pauline. *Creative Bookbinding.* University of Washington Press, 1973.
Lewis, A.W. *Basic Bookbinding.* Dover Publications, 1957.
Time/Life Books. *The Family Creative Workshop*, Volume 2, 230-243.

Self-actualization, which includes creativity, speculation, and innovation, is a "growth" need.—Lori Fisk/Henry Clay Lindgren, *Learning Centers*, 1974

Motivating Children to Read through Improved Self-Concept

Bonnie Deeds
Annunciation School
Cincinnati, Ohio

Children in our school systems are asked daily to take chances: to write a paper that will be evaluated, to read for a class that may laugh, to do board work that may be wrong, to create an object of art that will be judged. Viewed at another level, children are asked to risk their self-concept.

Canfield and Wells (6) draw a perfect analogy to illustrate this point. In the "poker chip theory of learning," the student's self-concept is a stack of poker chips. Some students start the learning game with a large stack of chips, and are able to sustain some losses. On the other hand, those students who begin with few chips suffer greatly with each loss. Because they risk being omitted from the game, the latter students will be much more cautious about taking chances. Thus, children who, for whatever reasons, have developed negative self-perceptions will be ready to accept themselves as inadequate learners as well. They are reticent about stepping out on a limb even though the limb might not break.

Learning to read is of particular concern with regard to this theory because of its critical importance to an individual. In a study of the effects of reading on groups of people, Waples (23) lists the prestige effect, reading for self-approval, second only to the functional effect. Thus, guiding learners toward successful reading experiences may help them to attain security and to approach other activities with confidence. If the chips are low, however, students may never realize this success. Therefore, there is an intricate interrelationship between a person's image of self and the ability to read.

Self-Concept Affects Reading

There are a number of carefully designed studies which clearly show that self-concept affects reading. Two separate studies, one by Lamy (15), the other by Wattenberg and Clifford (24), illustrate that measures of self-concept during kindergarten appear to be antecedent to and predictive of achievement. Toller (1968) compares self-evaluations of achieving readers with those of retarded readers. She found significant differences in favor of achievers on acceptance, adequacy, personal and social self, security, number of problems, and consistency of view of self. In 1967, Irwin (13) studied the self reports of freshman college students and reported significant relationships between reported self-concept and academic achievement. He summarized his research by stating, "It may well be that a positive concept of one's self as a person is not only more important than striving to get ahead and enthusiasm for studying and going to school, but that it is a central factor when considering optimal scholastic performance."

The conclusions seem unavoidable: Students carry with them certain attitudes about themselves and their abilities which play a primary role in how they perform in school. But the sword cuts both ways: scholastic performance directly influences self-concept.

Gibby and Gibby's studies (10) indicate that under the stress of a failure situation, academically superior students performed less effectively. Centi (7) proved in a similar study that this effect holds true for underachievers as well. Furthermore, Diggory (9) discovered that when one ability is important and highly rated (e.g. reading), a failure of that ability lowers one's self-evaluation of other, seemingly unrelated, abilities.

So the problem is intensified. Because there is a continuous interaction between the self and academic achievement, a vicious circle becomes established. Children who come to school believing they will not succeed in reading, as well as children who gain this concept at a later time, become victims of a self-fulfilling prophecy. Because they anticipate failure in reading, their behaviors and efforts during reading instruction contribute to making their expectations come true. And the student who has failed for other reasons will soon become disheartened, only to meet with successive failures.

As in all cyclical phenomena, a slowing down or even a complete arrest is difficult to precipitate. A second consideration, presented by Combes and Snygg (8), is that these perceptions of self satisfy a basic need. The dimension of the theory holds that the maintenance and enhancement of the perceived self is the motive behind all behavior. Therefore, perceptions which are consistent with that self are selected whether they appear complimentary or self-damaging to an outsider. Perceptions which are inconsistent are not likely to occur as they would not fit the self structure.

Several studies (1, 2) have shown that students who did poorly but expected to do so were more satisfied and contented than those who did well but had not expected to do so. Individuals are generally unwilling to accept evidence that is contrary to perceptions they hold of themselves, and they choose personal judgment over evidence when conflict arises. No matter how negative the self may be, who and what one is is most important, and anything is better than nothing at all.

So it is that the self resists change as much as possible in order to enjoy a consistent, organized world. However, the self (a view of self) will change if conditions are favorable. Snyder (22) expresses it this way: "The self concept is continually emerging ... It is never an established, fully structured product of the past, because with each situation in which the individual finds himself the self-concept is being created and re-created." Implicit in this statement is that by modifying the situation the individual's self-concept can be modified.

It might be mentioned here that some reluctant readers fall into separate, but related, categories. There are students, particularly among the socially disabled, who believe they have the ability to succeed but who view school as irrelevant, threatening, or both. If it is true that each of us is constantly striving to maintain, protect, and enhance the self of which we are aware, then it follows that experience is perceived in terms of its relevance to the self. The self is the individual's basic frame of reference. May (18) states: "We cannot ... stand outside our skin and perch on some Archimedes point and have a way of surveying experience that does not itself depend upon the assumptions that one makes about the nature of ... whatever one is studying." If instruction in school cannot be assimilated into the world of children, if it cannot be comprehended from their personal vantage points, no learning can take place.

So it has been established that poor self-concept is, in fact, detrimental to the student's ability to read, and that this image of self is difficult to erase. Therefore, it must first become a firm belief of the teacher that self-concept is an essential ingredient in the process of learning to read. The educator must add a second dimension to reading. Just as word attack, vocabulary building, and recognition skills are basic to successful reading so, too, is a positive self image. It is the task of the teacher, then, to provide ways for the student to gain a positive and realistic self-image as a learner, as a reader.

An underlying factor in the establishment of a pleasing self is the attitude of the teacher. A basic assumption of the theory of the self-concept is that we behave according to our beliefs. If this assumption is true, then it follows that teachers' beliefs about themselves and their students are crucial factors in determining the effectiveness of teaching. Brookover and associates (5) confirmed that improved self-concepts result from the expectations and evaluations held by significant others (teachers, parents, friends) as perceived by the student. This, again, confirms the self-fulfilling prophecy, but in relation to the teacher. Successful reading, then, begins not with procedures, but with creative, perceptive teachers who believe children want to learn.

Second, teachers must take steps to try to sense how individuals view themselves. Only then can teachers develop ways to improve this image. This is not an easy task, for you cannot really see things from other's points of view until you climb into their skins. But the task can be facilitated by administering self-report inventories such as the Self-Esteem Inventory, the Bledsoe Self-Concept Scale, the Q-Sort, and the Self-Appraisal Scale. Since we can't be sure students have responded truthfully, personal observations that can be inferred from student behavior can be most effective. It must be kept in mind that students' perceptions of their appearance and behavior are more important to our understanding of the students than are their appearance and behavior in themselves.

Improving Self-Image

Once teachers have assessed the situation, the most important task to be faced is that of providing students with ways to improve their self-images. Canfield and Wells, in a book entitled "100 Ways to Enhance Self-Concept in the Classroom" (*6*), list explicitly and concisely various exercises that focus on this task. The book covers such areas as accepting your body, realizing strengths, knowing yourself, and building an environment of positive support. Use of this tool in a curriculum would undoubtedly provide a strong foundation for building self-esteem.

Perhaps the single most important step in restoring a shattered ego is to provide repeated experiences of success. It is on this idea that the remainder of the paper will focus. Just as research shows that failure in an ability that is rated as important leads to a lower self-evaluation of other abilities, the converse is also true. Success in an area highly rated by self will result in a feeling of higher potential in other areas. Wylie (*25*) concludes that students are likely to change their self-evaluation after experimentally induced success or failure. Personal experience is also testimony to the elated feelings caused by a triumphant experience. We must bear in mind the fact that this change will not occur too quickly due to the preservation of self.

Since reading has been an area of failure for some children, therefore a weakening to their self-image, it does not follow to continue to present exercises in reading alone. Students will be most reluctant to attempt tasks in which they've had no previous success; the educational wounds must first heal. So the teacher must capitalize on children's strengths in any area and create meaningful experiences in which the children can prove their capabilities to themselves.

It has long been recognized that usually the most effective method of teaching children is individually. This is a sound procedure from both psychological and educational points of view. The objective of the individualized approach is the fullest development of the student's skills and capacities through methods commensurate to the learning style of the child. Traditional methods have obviously failed for the reluctant reader. We need to zero in on what works for this student. The formula, then, is to involve students in something both successful and relevant to their world.

In order to provide experiences that have personal meaning, the teacher must be concerned with children's interests. In most cases, these can be easily detected. But some of these children may see themselves as helpless, without any well-defined goals, and unable to make decisions. So it becomes necessary to stimulate them through new ideas and guide them to discover their potentials.

It has been observed repeatedly that many nonreaders are highly proficient in other areas. Einstein, for example, had repeated failures in language related areas, but had a highly developed sense of visual imagery. A biographer of Einstein made the following comment: "It is coming to be more widely agreed that an apparent defect in a particular person may merely indicate an imbalance in our normal expectations. A noted deficiency should alert us to look for a proficiency of a different kind in the exceptional person. The late use of language in childhood, the difficulty in learning foreign languages ... may indicate a polarization or displacement in some of the skill to another area" (11).

In the dyslexic student, the left hemisphere of the brain, the language center, may be underdeveloped. Levy (16) suggests that one side of the brain develops at the expense of the other. This would mean that in the dyslexic child, the right side, which controls spatial orientation functions, would be highly developed. Through its superior correlative skills, the right hemisphere is more synthetic and manipulative in its mode of thought. It is looked upon by some as the more imaginative and creative feature of the brain (17). Putting together models, repairing things, and finding their way around are second nature to these children. They often possess a keen artistic ability, due to their creativity and acute awareness of the space around them in terms of distance, form, direction, and position.

Build on Children's Interests

So why not capitalize on these abilities? It's a gross injustice of our educational system to continually remind nonreaders of their downfall. Even though they may do little else well, readers are "good," nonreaders are "bad." Give students repeated instances to prove their worth, and they will slowly begin to change the deflated images they have carried for years; they need more than just encouraging words and a pat on the back. It would be more effective to involve nonreaders in a project over a period of time, affording them opportunities to develop a latent interest or gain a new one.

Many of these children have some kind of artistic ability and, even if they are not proficient, they need the opportunity to express themselves and to feel comfortable with their expressions. I am proposing some methods of using the fine arts from which to gain a successful, meaningful experience. Reading can be an integral part of the project, but it must be stressed that students shouldn't be forced to read. This must be a positive experience. In some cases, reading is only incidental. Children will want to read more in reference to their projects; reading then becomes relevant to their interests and not a separate entity. These projects overlap in some ways. Keep in mind that they are just starting points from which to build children's interests.

Photography

Through photography children can express themselves even if they feel deficient as an artist. It is particularly good if one has access to a darkroom. Then the children are responsible for each step, so gratification will be greater. If a darkroom is not available, children still can be active in taking pictures and selecting those that please them. If they do not have access to a camera, it is possible to make a simplified camera from an oatmeal box (see *Hocus Focus* in the list of books).

First, allow the children to photograph any subjects to determine where their interests lie. Develop this interest. If they bring in pictures of friends and family, discuss ways to photograph people—candid versus posed, action versus still shots, capturing expressions and feelings. Introduce photographers who focus on people and discuss their intent. The scientific and artistic elements of photography can be integrated, using books as an aid, if the children are old enough to grasp these concepts. Magazines can be used to further explore photographs. If the children continue to show interest, ask them to put together a family "portrait," using the pictures to illustrate a theme such as "A day in the life...," "Family Interaction," etc. Written captions would help to convey the message.

Next use photographs to illustrate a favorite story, limiting the setting to the school neighborhood. This allows use of imagination and also shows the dynamics of photography (double exposure, intentional blurs). Or a group can compose a science fiction story and then illustrate it. Assuming the role of news reporters, they could do a feature article on the school or neighborhood.

It would be most prestigious to involve the students in a photography display related to the school. If the school is trying to improve behavior in the cafeteria, for example, the students can be assigned to photograph examples of good and poor behavior and make posters to illustrate. They could do publicity for a play or talent show. Perhaps they could do a feature story on a classmate for the school paper.

As interest grows, continue to present books on photography so the students begin to feel that not all books are their enemies.

Cartoons

Nearly every child loves comic books. And those who like to draw often draw comic book characters. Boys especially identify with the super heroes from the comic strips. If students like to read only comic books, allow them to read comic books. Reading is reading.

Ask students to create their own super heroes/heroines. What can they do? How would they fit in our society? Compare to other story/comic book heroes to help develop the character. This activity would offer an opportunity to introduce books. There are many low readability stories in comic books. Begin to develop a story around the hero. Ask the children to illustrate the story, or perhaps only the ending of the story, just as if it were a page in a comic book. Allow time to include detailed pictures if desired; provide drawing books as aids. If children have difficulties in creating characters, they may be asked to do a sequel to a favorite comic strip. If they choose one that appears in story form in the daily newspaper, check the next day to see how close their predictions were to the newspaper strip. This activity could then become a take off point for reading instruction.

If students are interested in developing their styles, introduce them to famous illustrators and look for their works in other books. Artists who draw the world of fantasy are particularly interesting to some. A project using various styles to illustrate one thing could be developed. Caricatures may be of interest to others. Show examples in magazines and discuss their use. Have students draw a caricature of someone they like and someone they're not so fond of. They may want to do students and teachers to be posted in the hall, again giving the children recognition.

Animation

Animation can be a take off from either photography or comic strips, but can involve other art forms as well. This is a project in which each student takes an active and important part in the process. The production could be likened to that of Hollywood, with the teacher assigning a director, producer, and cameraperson. Scenes in the story can be a combination of real life photography, drawings, and three dimensional figures. A soundtrack could easily be made to accompany the story. Emphasize that the student playing each role is perfect for that part for a particular reason. By naming each student in the credits, student accomplishment is being reinforced. The project, of course, can be done on a lesser scale with only one individual.

Drawing

Students who use a more realistic approach to drawing will probably want to learn to improve their techniques. For this reason, drawing books will be readily accepted. Students may be interested not only in how to draw the human figure, for example, but also in the artistic elements that comprise a good drawing. There are various books on an intermediate level that show the basics of design, color, form, shading, and perspective. When using drawing books for reading instruction, students should be allowed to draw just as frequently as they read.

Since we are aiming to build the child's confidence, in any given project the drawing end should be the central factor. Take for example students who like to draw animals. Don't ask students to compare the lion and tiger in writing, but focus on showing characteristics through pictures. Students could, through a number of illustrations, compare animals in appearance and social habits. Some reading will be necessary, but the teacher should facilitate this as much as possible. The end product would be some large, impressive drawings with only little writing.

If children like to draw, doing self-portraits could be fun. They might want to do a series at different ages, projecting into the years ahead. Or they may want to draw themselves in different settings, showing typical days in their lives. Encourage them to change their expressions with each event, enabling them to tune in to their feelings.

Calligraphy

The idea behind teaching calligraphy is that even if students don't become accomplished calligraphers, their writing can still be made to look special. Because the materials are relatively inexpensive, the teacher could use the supplies to reward students for certain desirable behaviors. As the students progress, they could become known as the school's calligraphers; teachers and students should be encouraged to use these students when special work is needed.

A List of Books in the Fine Arts

The Real Book about Photography, William Gottlieb, Garden City Books.
The Boys' Book of Photography, Edwin Teale. E.P. Dutton.
Photography with the Basic Camera, William Gottlieb. Alfred A. Knopf.
What Does a Photographer Do? T. Mergendahl. Dodd, Mead.
The First Book of Photography, John Hoke. Watts.
Lens and Shutter: An Introduction to Photography, Harvey Weiss. Young Scott Books.
Great Photographers. Time-Life Books.
The 35mm Portrait, Jack Manning. Amphoto (American Photography Book Publishing).
Photo Fun: An Idea Book for Shutterbugs, David Webster. Franklin Watts.
Hocus Focus: The World's Weirdest Cameras, Carl Glassman. Franklin Watts.
The Photographer's Handbook, John Hedgecoe. Alfred A. Knopf.
Discovering Design, Marion Downer. Lothrop, Lee, and Shepard.
The Graphic Word of M.C. Escher. Ballantine Books.
Fantastic Art of Frank Frazetta. Peacock Press.

More Shapes and Stories, Geoffrey and Jane Grigson. Vanguard.
Art is Everywhere, Leonard Kessler. Dodd, Mead.
Posters: Designing, Making, and Reproducing, George Horn. Davis.
Humorous Drawing Made Easy, Doug Anderson. Sterling.
Comic Book of Pets, Arnold Roth. Charles Scribner's Sons.
The Art of David Levine. Alfred A. Knopf.
Masterpieces of Science Fiction Art: Tomorrow and Beyond, Ian Summers.
Art for Children Series, Ernest Raboff. Doubleday.
The Pantheon Story of American Art for Young People, Arianne Batterberry.
How to Draw Athletes in Action, Arthur Zaidenburg. Abelard-Schuman.
Getting Started in Film Making, Lillian Schiff. Sterling.
Make Your Own Animated Movies, Y. Anderson. Little, Brown.
Fun Time Radio and Movie Productions, Cameron Yerian.

References

1. ARONSON, E., and J. MILLS. "The Affects of Severity of Initiation on Liking for a Group," *Journal of Abnormal and Social Psychology*, 59 (1959), 177-181.
2. ARONSON, E., and J.M. CARLSMITH. "Performance Expectancy as a Determinant of Actual Performance," *Journal of Abnormal and Social Psychology*, 65 (1962), 178-182.
3. BARBE, WALTER B. *Educator's Guide to Personalized Reading Instruction*. Englewood Cliffs, New Jersey: Prentice-Hall, 1961.
4. BERRETA, SHIRLEY C. "Self-Concept Development in the Reading Program," *Reading Teacher*, 24 (December 1970), 232-238.
5. BROOKOVER, W.B. "Self-Concept of Ability and School Achievement," *Sociology of Education*, 37 (1964), 271-278.
6. CANFIELD, JACK, and HAROLD C. WELLS. *100 Ways to Enhance Self-Concept in the Classroom*. Englewood Cliffs, New Jersey: Prentice-Hall, 1976.
7. CENTI, P. "Self-Perception of Students and Motivation," *Catholic Educational Review*, 63 (1965), 307-319.
8. COMBS, A.W., and D. SNYGG. *Individual Behavior*. New York: Harper and Row, 1959.
9. DIGGORY, J.C. *Self-Evaluation: Concepts and Studies*. New York: John Wiley and Sons, 1966.
10. GIBBY, R.G., SR., and R.G. GIBBY, JR. "The Effects of Stress Resulting from Academic Failures," *Journal of Clincial Psychology*, 23 (1967), 35-37.
11. HOLTON, G. "On Trying to Understand Scientific Genius," *American Scholar*, 41 (1971-1972), 102.
12. HOMZE, ALMA C. "Reading and the Self-Concept," *Elementary English*, 39 (March 1962), 210.
13. IRWIN, F.S. "Sentence Completion Responses and Scholastic Success or Failure," *Journal of Counselling Psychology*, 14 (1967), 269-271.
14. JASON, MARTIN H., and BEATRICE DUBNOW. "The Relationship between Self-Perceptions of Reading Abilities and Reading Achievement," in Walter H. MacGinitie (Ed.), *Assessment Problems in Reading*. Newark, Delaware: International Reading Association, 1973.
15. LAMY, M.W. "Relationship of Self-Perceptions of Early Primary Children to Achievement in Reading," in I.J. Gordon (Ed.), *Human Development: Readings in Research*. Chicago: Scott, Foresman, 1965.

16. LEVY, J. "Possible Basis for the Evolution of Lateral Specialization of the Human Brain, *Nature*, 224 (1969), 614-615.
17. MASLAND, RICHARD L. "The Advantages of Being Dyslexic," Orton Society Reprint Series, No. 72. Towson, Maryland, 1976.
18. MAY, R. *Man's Search for Himself*. New York: W.W. Norton, 1953.
19. NOLAND, RONALD G. "Methods to Motivate Reluctant Readers," *Journal of Reading*, 19 (February 1976), 387-392.
20. PURKEY, WILLIAM W. *Self-Concept and School Achievement*. Englewood Cliffs, New Jersey: Prentice-Hall, 1970.
21. SANACORE, JOSEPH. "Reading Self-Concept: Assessment and Enhancement," *Reading Teacher*, 29 (November 1975), 164-168.
22. SNYDER, ELDON E. "Self-Concept Theory: An Approach to Understanding the Behavior of Disadvantaged Pupils," *Clearing House*, 40 (December 1965), 242-246.
23. WAPLES, DOUGLAS. *What Reading Does to People*. Chicago: University of Chicago Press, 1940.
24. WATTENBURG, WILLIAM W., and CLARE CLIFFORD. "Relation of Self-Concept to Beginning Achievement in Reading," *Child Psychology*, 35 (June 1964), 461-467.
25. WYLIE, R.C. *The Self-Concept: A Critical Survey of Pertinent Research Literature*. Lincoln: University of Nebraska Press, 1961.

Improving Self-Concept

Obviously reading is a visual activity, in the sense that we cannot read print with the lights out.—Frank Smith, *Psycholinguistics and Reading*, 1973

Lights, Camera, Action! The Camera as a Tool for Teaching Reading

Victoria Miller Waller
University of California at Los Angeles

It seems that the use of television and film as a teaching tool in the classroom has received much criticism. Primarily, this negative attitude towards this medium is attributed to its passive nature. Bruner (1966) characterizes the nature of intellectual growth as contingent upon an interaction between the learner and the stimulus. Thus, merely observing a stimulus without any feedback mechanism, as in watching TV or films, would not present the optimal result. However, learner participation would seem to provide the interaction necessary for intellectual growth. The process of structuring this active participation with the appropriate motivation then becomes the responsibility of the teacher. This task can be greatly facilitated by engaging students in the active role of creating their own films and picture stories as a means of securing their participation in a total language program.

The article which follows will provide information on raising money to buy equipment, offer ideas for the use of photos and slides in your classroom, and discuss some skills practiced while using cameras in the classroom. It is hypothesized that, through the use of cameras in the classroom, the teacher is able to motivate even the most reluctant readers.

A True Story

A group of sixth grade boys in a "special" reading class were overheard to say, "The only play I've ever been in was in third grade.... I was a tree." "We can't read. How can we be in a play?" These sixth graders proceeded to write, direct, produce, take slides of, and star in a play about a "Hamburglar" who steals hamburgers from McDonald's Restaurant. French Fry Spy was called in to solve the case, which he did, by putting diet pickles in the Hamburglar's hamburgers so that the thief lost his appetite and did not steal anymore. Permission was granted for the boys to film on location at McDonald's. A project with cameras was born and students became excited about learning and knowing how to read.

Funding Your Project

Raising money for your project(s) is the hardest step. Most school systems do not have money for camera projects, so it is up to the teacher to arrange money making ventures. Following are some starter ideas. Try these or variations to secure funding.

1. *Have a book sale.* Students in school bring books from home for sale to other students. This is a good project for Book Week in November. Students sort the books brought in according to subject and grade levels, which in itself is a valuable reading-learning experience. Part of the profits from the book sale goes to the class that brings in the most books.

2. *Make a newspaper.* Students write stories about class and other school activities. Column ideas might include "Dear Blabby" or topics such as latest fashions, tongue twisters, and sports. Sale of the paper to other students raises funds for your camera projects.

3. *Have each student contract to earn a certain amount of money.*

4. *Have a white elephant sale at a parent-teacher meeting.*

5. *Have each student do an art project.* Invite the parents to an auction of the art work.

6. *Have a talent show.* Sell tickets.

7. *Have each parent contribute favorite recipe(s).* Compile a recipe book to be sold.

8. *Have a "Gong Show."* Enlist acts from the entire school. Sell tickets to the event.

Remember: All money making ventures should be cleared by the principal and/or parents. Also, owners of camera shops receive tax deductions on merchandise given to schools (new cameras, used cameras that have been traded in, film, film processing) so it is possible to approach them for contributions.

A Collection of Project Ideas

The following are camera projects to make for the use of photos and slides in your classroom. Projects to make:

1. *Photo albums.* The cover is made of cardboard or construction paper in any shape chosen by the student (cat, tree, camera). The inside pages, cut in the same shape as the cover, have a story illustrated with the photos taken by the students, or students may just use photos with captions. Use photo corners for the mounting of pictures.

2. *Books.* Use construction paper or cardboard covered with material for the book covers. Students write original stories using their photos as illustrations. Pages can be secured in the book by staples or yarn strung through holes.

3. *Pull down photo stories.* A photo is glued onto cardboard. The cardboard can be any shape a student wishes. The student then writes a story about the photo on construction paper. A slit is made in the cardboard and the story is pulled down to be read.

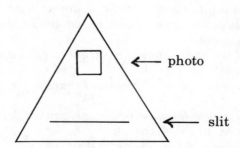

4. *Shoebox slide projectors.* Students write stories about their photos. Each story with photos is put on one long piece of cardboard. A peephole is put in one end of a shoebox. The top of the box has two slits. One large slit allows light to

shine through. Parallel slits are made through the bottom and the top of the box, allowing the story to slide through. The shoebox can be covered with material.

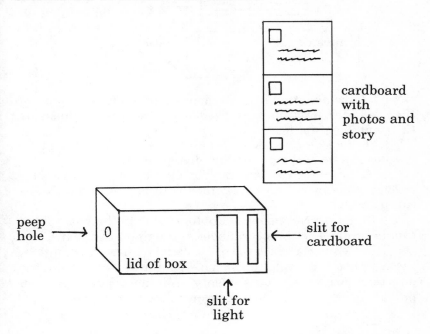

cardboard with photos and story

peep hole →

slit for cardboard ←

lid of box

↑ slit for light

5. *TV shoeboxes*. A shoebox can be made to look like a TV by standing the shoebox on its side and cutting a rectangle on the lid. Slits are cut on the long sides of the shoebox. The story with accompanying photos is pasted on a roll of paper that will pull through the slits in the shoebox. Knobs and antenna can be made for the TV.

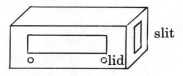

slit

lid

6. *Photo dioramas*. The shoebox stands on its side, and the lid with the story glued on it, is pasted on the top. The photos, illustrating the story, are pasted inside. Students may

want to add a 3D effect by placing small objects or cutouts in front of the photographs.

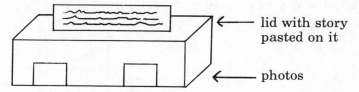

7. *Autobiographies*. Students can include photos of their families, environment, friends, and schools to illustrate their autobiographies.

8. *Biographies*. A biography of a pet, best friend, or teacher can be accompanied by photographs.

9. *Science experiments*. The step by step process of a science experiment can be recorded with photos and captions can be attached.

10. *Photo scrapbooks*. Photographs of class or school events can be kept in a scrapbook throughout the year.

Remember, the degree of success you have with any of these projects in your own classroom will depend on the direction you give your students and the opportunity you provide for them to pursue their own ideas.

A Total Language Approach

The following ideas will provide suggestions for integrating the language arts in your classroom.

1. *Sequencing*. Take a field trip through the neighborhood or park. Photograph scenes along the way. In the classroom the students can put the photos in sequential order.

Tape record a script to accompany photographs. Students then can match photographs to the description on tape, following the sequence they hear.

2. *Labelling*. Have students plan photo settings including different objects which are labelled and ask them to make photos or slides of the settings (chairs, tables, nose, ears). Students then can match objects to settings. Labelling can be related to the students' interests, such as sports cars, various animals, or favorite foods.

3. *Vocabulary expansion.* Use familiar symbols to teach skills and vocabulary, such as a fire box, street sign, or cereal box.

4. *Evoking feelings.* Show that the same photo can evoke different feelings. For example, take a picture of a person getting weighed. Tape record two responses to the photo or slide. "My, you've lost weight." or "Oh dear, you've gained weight."

5. *Matching.* Ask students to make up a play and take slides of it. Then a tape recording of the script can be matched to the slides.

6. *Alphabetizing.* Suggest that older students take photographs or slides illustrating every letter of the alphabet. Each slide can be matched to a tape recorded sentence. Younger students can listen to the tape and see the accompanying slides.

7. *Photo journalism.* Help students make photos for a class newspaper. The fashion page could have photos of students modeling the latest fashions and be accompanied by a written story. Similar projects can be done with every area of the newspaper.

8. *Thought communication.* Photos or slides can show how we communicate our thoughts and feelings in ways other than with our hands (such as photos of people with different facial expressions or different body positions). Ask the students to identify the emotions expressed in various photos.

9. *Interpretation.* Suggest that students switch photos they have taken and then write a title or a story for each photo.

10. *Vocabulary expansion.* Ask students to take photos illustrating their interests and write 50 vocabulary words that are shown or implied. Students can then share their lists with others and perhaps gain new words which can be added to the list.

11. *Photo exchange.* Help students exchange photos and stories about their school with students in another school.

12. *Photo debate.* Have students hold a photo debate (one group can argue pro, one can argue con). Each group can take photos to help win their argument.

13. *Media interpretation.* Divide the class into two groups. One group takes positive photos of the school; the other

group takes negative photos of the school. Show the two sets of slides of the same activity or setting. Then have a discussion on media interpretation. "Should you believe everything you see on TV?"

14. *Ordering.* Ask students to place a series of photographs of an activity in the correct order (e.g., cooking, car repair, building a model).

15. *Captioning.* Have students write captions or stories to go with photos. Conversely, each student is given a title and then chooses a photo to go with it.

16. *Creative writing.* Place a student's photo on the board. Have others write a story to describe the photo or create an advertisement about it.

17. *Observing details.* Ask students to look at a photo one minute, cover the photo, and then write down the details. Or ask them to choose two photos and explain how they are alike and why.

18. *Information gathering and compiling.* Help students compile a consumer and resource guide for their neighborhood. Students can find out what items are sold in the stores, the addresses of the stores, describe parking facilities, and record the names of the managers. The students can compile, print, and distribute the information. (This project can also be a money raiser.)

19. *Brainstorming.* Place student's photo or project a slide on the wall and ask students to name all the words the photo brings to mind.

20. *Role definition.* Ask students to take photos depicting different sex roles (someone working with tools, cooking, etc.). Follow with a discussion.

21. *Reading enhancement.* Have students take photos or slides to enhance the reading of everyday material (medicine bottles, parking meters, etc.).

All of these activities should be viewed as starters. As you try them, you can add or delete activities as best fits your own classroom needs.

Some Skills Worth Reinforcing

All activities defined in this chapter involve reading and language skills. The list of skills used while working with photos and slides are:

1. Word Attack Skills
2. Literal Comprehension Skills
   sequencing
   main idea
   recalling details
   following directions
   retelling stories
   recalling previous events
   illustrating stories
   relating picture and title
   finding specific information
3. Interpretive Comprehension
   interpreting character motives and feelings
   sensing emotional overtones
   making deductions, judgments, drawing conclusions
   organizing, summarizing
   interpreting pictures
   contrasting and comparing
   predicting story events

Lights, Camera, Action!

The camera is a valuable tool for creative teaching of reading skills; at the same time, there is the opportunity to build student self-confidence and a love for reading. If our responsibility as teachers is to stimulate students to want to read instead of thinking of reading as a duty, then the use of cameras will certainly provide a helpful step in this direction. Smile!

Discovery also implies experimentation and investigation, and a learning center can be made a place in which children can examine and test their own ideas without the need to feel defensive or apologetic about them.—Lori Fisk/Henry Clay Lindgren, *Learning Centers,* 1974

Reading Lab or Resource Room: What Services Can Be Provided?

Connie Porter
Seven Hills Upper School
Cincinnati, Ohio

Within the framework of a reading laboratory or resource room, it *is* possible to help reluctant readers (who most likely are also underachievers) with effective, individually designed support systems. Such systems seek not only to determine the sources of reluctance to read, but also to provide the experiences needed for growth in areas such as language development, reading skill development, study skills, and motivation to help students overcome their apparent distaste for reading.

Once the funds are available to equip such a lab or room, the quality or degree of success with students depends largely upon three ingredients: the capabilities of an intellectually and emotionally sound teacher, the support of the faculty and administration, and the element of flexibility. Given the current controversy regarding the "meaning" of a high school diploma, it is necessary to state explicitly, at this point, one major assumption which is essential for the success of such a support system: it is assumed that the school itself, in all sectors, is faithfully demanding a competency in reading skills appropriate to the child's intellectual capacity before granting its credentials, credits, and diploma. Without a standard to reach for, it becomes nearly impossible to motivate the students to improve their skills, and without motivation, the resource room or reading lab is an expensive exercise in futility.

Three Key Ingredients

First of all, it is absolutely necessary to engage a person to assume responsibility for directing the lab or resource room, one who is both stimulating and creative intellectually and who is well-balanced and secure emotionally. Specifically, this instructor *must* have a working, usable knowledge of the English language system: its nature and history, how it is acquired, what problems may occur in the development of various phases of receptive and expressive language, how to detect these problems accurately, and what may be done to overcome or compensate for the problems as the child matures. It is equally essential that the instructor be able to recognize a child's insecurities, frustrations, and feelings of inadequacy and, with mature insight, help that child to cope. Creative solutions to troublesome problems, sought out with positive, genuinely caring attitudes, lead to amazing "success stories" in the lab.

Another key to a useful lab or resource room is a network of adminsitrative and faculty support. Without the principal and teachers to encourage parents and students to view and refer to the resource room in positive ways, the stigma of "needing help" often remains an insurmountable obstacle. Equally important are department chairpersons who encourage their teachers to view the lab as an extension of their own classes. Needless to say, administrative backing for financial support to keep the instructor current in research, methodology, and materials keeps morale high and encourages a steady flow of creative energies and fresh ideas.

The third ingredient to a successful lab or resource room is flexibility. First of all, the schedule must be flexible enough to allow the student time (preferably out of a study hall and not out of a class he enjoys) to add reading lab to his schedule without sacrifice. The attitude of the administration needs to be flexible in granting the teacher the latitude she/he needs in designing programs, ordering equipment and supplies, and encouraging faculty input and collaboration. Most of all, the *teacher* must be a very flexible person; able to adjust daily programs to meet unexpected needs; able to react appropriately to the unpredictable moods of young adolescents; and able, by means of sound diagnostic teaching, to redesign a long-term program quickly to match the growth and newly unfolding needs of the participant.

Components of the System
Diagnostic Procedures

For descriptive purposes the support system breaks down easily into three major components: diagnostic procedures, program planning and implementation, and evaluation. Before any formal testing begins, time must be provided for informal, private discussions in a relaxed atmosphere to establish some kind of rapport and trust between student and instructor. It may be assumed, for the time being, that the student's reluctance to read masks some real problems in his reading behavior. The goals of these diagnostic sessions are to draw working hypotheses concerning the underlying problem(s). During these first (one or two) informal sessions, the following areas are useful topics for discussion at the appropriate time: the student's reading habits, what he knows about his own reading behavior, his current attitude and feelings about reading, his early experiences with reading, his interests, how he uses time at home and in school, and his perception of his learning patterns in school and at home. In reality, it may take many months before most of these and other relevant topics have been touched; however, the investment of time and patience is fruitful because much insight, as well as mutual confidence, is gained from this shared self-knowledge. The child has "owned" these problems for some time now and should be encouraged to verbalize what he has been experiencing.

Once insight and rapport have been established, some of the more formal assessments of language skills may be undertaken. The student's spoken language (ideally observed in a variety of social settings) and samples of his written language, including a standardized spelling test, will provide clues for the level of development of his expressive language.

Informal and standardized diagnostic tests of listening and reading comprehension offer some data for assessing receptive language skills. If any intelligence test is to be used, the most useful are those which are administered individually and which attempt to assess some thinking skills without relying on the student's reading skills (i.e. the WISC or the WAIS, depending on the age of the student). In addition to revealing significant disparities between verbal and performance skills, the subtests can be especially useful clues to the strengths and weaknesses in the visual and auditory channels for processing and retrieving information. The instructor must also have easy access to the permanent record file, teachers' observations and parental input. Since the odds are quite high that the student's past experiences with standardized tests have been mostly negative, limiting these tests to the bare minimum during the early stages of diagnosis is preferable. Regardless of the number or the nature of the tests used, the point to be underscored here is that this initial diagnostic experience should provide the opportunity to establish rapport and to begin to build realistic expectations for predictable areas of growth. It is obvious that with time and human limitations, it would be impossible to gather all the diagnostic information needed during this initial stage. Therefore, diagnosis must be considered an on-going process which is incorporated into the daily teaching-learning processes, whereby initial hypotheses are either verified or eventually discarded and replaced.

Program Planning and Implementation

With the formation of some initial hypotheses, it is time to plan the program *with* the student. Logically this is also the time to share appropriately these hypotheses with the student in order to build a sound rationale for his program. For planning purposes, a list of areas for possible exploration may be helpful. The areas which seem to be most crucial to both teacher and student can be checked off for immediate attention, while noting other areas for later consideration. A typical list could also include space to designate materials and evaluation methods to be used and might resemble the following:

AREA FOR WORK	MATERIALS TO USE	INDICATORS OF PROGRESS
1. Improving comprehension		
2. Improving spelling		
3. Broadening vocabulary		
4. Improving study habits		
5. Strengthening test taking skills		
6. Improving knowledge of grammar, usage, punctuation		
7. Improving word analysis skills		
8. Other (i.e., handwriting)		

Once these specific areas have been identified, a daily plan of activities can be worked out with the student. Then he is ready to begin his regularly scheduled sessions (minimum of three times per week). The goal at this point is to have the student know *what* he is doing in these sessions, *why* he is doing this particular activity, and *how* he initiates and carries out the activity successfully. Whenever possible, most of the work can be connected immediately by the student himself. Some of his work is done individually. Some of it is done in small groups. His daily activity plans are guidelines so that he will know what is expected of him. However, these plans are not rigid; the student knows (or will come to know) that if there is a pressing academic problem or a difficult assignment from a course, he can seek help with confidence in the lab. It is *vitally* important to instill student awareness of the link between the work done in the lab and the work he is being asked to do in his classes. Bringing in tests and graded papers is one more way in which the student takes part in monitoring his progress.

Success breeds more success, so with prudent guidance the instructor must arrange for immediate success experiences within the first few sessions in the lab. She/he might do this, for example, by showing the student some simple steps in how to study for a vocabulary or spelling test, using a card system, an association-memory trick, or an analysis of the structure of words (if the student is ready for that). Once there has been a "crack in the wall" of reluctance to read, the teacher should be ready to provide the wedge by allowing the student precious time in the lab to read, especially if *he* asks to do so. The lab, of course, must be amply supplied with a large variety of books and magazines readily available for student use. Sometimes, the controlled reader, used with an appropriate level and speed, can spark the interest of a slow reader when he discovers he really can understand what he has read at a slightly faster pace. For another student a world of insight unfolds as he grasps the significance of the syllabic structure of words and a phonic key for figuring out those "long" words he knows by sound but not by sight; the impact of this discovery can leave him virtually like "putty" in the hands of a competent teacher. Then, of course, there are always those students (especially the older ones) who resist, to the end, any acknowledgement of a "problem with reading" but who will accept help with spelling only. With this type of student, it may be possible to slip in the back door by agreeing to help him. As he discovers the phonetic and structural nature of the English spelling system, as well as how to cope with its peculiarities, he may gradually be encouraged to take a closer look at his reading strategies. The approaches to the problems of the "reluctant reader" are as infinite and open-ended as the imagination and creativity of the teacher.

Evaluation

There is no formal grading procedure, as such, in this support system although the report card may indicate that the student is involved in such a program. However, evaluation of progress takes place on several fronts: immediate daily feedback from self-corrected work; frequent informal (lab) teacher feedback and interpretation of daily work results; informal feedback from teachers who see signs of academic progress; improved letter grades in course; and an individual conference in June to interpret May standardized testing results, self-evaluation and other evaluative data. When possible, a formal written evaluation is compiled by the lab or resource teacher and sent home in June.

Even when all of the ingredients are there for a good reading lab or resource room, every student will not be a "success story." People who do not *enjoy* reading may someday, if we are lucky, be accepted the same way we accept people who do not like to sing or people who do not like to play tennis. If the school and the instructor can face and accept this hard reality, then it is possible to move on to experience incredible joy in what actually *does happen* to improve the lot of many people with reading problems. What greater joy than to have a former student rush up with the latest best-seller that he has just read and burst out with, "You just have to read this!"

0